Keeping our Children Safe from sexual predators

In the community and on-line
A Must Know - A Need to Know:

MC Griffin Campbell, MA, M.Div.
Children of Victory, Founder/President
www.childrenofvictory.com

Keeping our Children Safe from sexual predators

A Special "Appreciation and Thanks" to: My husband, Gene who has always been my #1 Cheerleader and supporter, children, grand children, great grandchild and supporters of Child Safety.

To the families of all "Missing & Exploited Children", please know that you are not forgotten. We are here for you.

Community Partnerships, appreciation for your support:

1. NCMEC, National Center for Missing and Exploited Children.
2. Federal Law Enforcement Agencies: Robert Mueller, Director FBI & FBI, Los Angeles
3. US Marshal office, Los Angeles
4. Los Angeles County Sheriff Department, Sheriff Lee Baca
5. LAPD, Chief Charlie Beck
6. Los Angeles County Probation Department
7. Los Angeles County Board of Supervisor, Mike Antonovich
8. Los Angeles City Council, Tom LaBonge
9. Los Angeles City Council, Jan Perry

"The test of the morality of a society is what it does for its children."
~Dietrich Bonhoeffer

Keeping our Children Safe from sexual predators

Keeping our Children Safe from predators is a top priority. A part of keeping our children safe is to be Child Safety educated, informed and empowered. Always keeping in mind:

1. The risk is great.
2. Our children are depending on us to keep them safe.
3. The predators are out there also, therefore, we must be Child Safety educated, trained and empowered to better protect our children.
4. "Awareness is our best Defense."
5. Working together protects children

"The only thing necessary for the triumph of evil is for good people to do nothing." Edmund Burke

Child Safety Overview: What is Child Abuse?

Each State provides its own definitions of child abuse and neglect based on minimum standards set by Federal law.

How Is Child Abuse and Neglect Defined in Federal Law?

Federal legislation lays the groundwork for States by identifying a minimum set of acts or behaviors that define child abuse and neglect.

The Federal Child Abuse Prevention and Treatment Act (CAPTA), (42 U.S.C.A. §5106g), as amended by the Keeping Children and

Keeping our Children Safe from sexual predators

Families Safe Act of 2003 defines child abuse and neglect as, at minimum:

- Any recent act or failure to act on the part of a parent or caretaker which results in death, serious physical or emotional harm, sexual abuse or exploitation.
- An act or failure to act which presents an imminent risk of serious harm.

Most Federal and State child protection laws primarily refer to cases of harm to a child caused by parents or other caregivers; they generally do not include harm caused by other people, such as acquaintances or strangers.

What Are the Major Types of Child Abuse and Neglect?

Within the minimum standards set by CAPTA, each State is responsible for providing its own definitions of child abuse and neglect. Most States recognize four major types of maltreatment: physical abuse, neglect, sexual abuse, and emotional abuse. Although any of the forms of child maltreatment may be found separately, they often occur in combination. In many States, abandonment and parental substance abuse are also defined as forms of child abuse or neglect.

The examples provided below are for general informational purposes only. Not all States' definitions will include all of the examples listed below, and individual States' definitions may cover additional situations not mentioned here.

Physical abuse is non accidental physical injury (ranging from minor bruises to severe fractures or death) as a result of punching, beating, kicking, biting, shaking, throwing, stabbing, choking, hitting (with a hand, stick, strap, or other object), burning, or otherwise harming a child, that is inflicted by a parent, caregiver, or other person who has responsibility for the child. Such injury is considered abuse regardless of whether the caregiver intended to hurt the child. Physical discipline, such as spanking or paddling, is not considered abuse as long as it is reasonable and causes no bodily injury to the child.

Neglect is the failure of a parent, guardian, or other caregiver to provide for a child's basic needs. Neglect may be:

- Physical (e.g., failure to provide necessary food or shelter, or lack of appropriate supervision)
- Medical (e.g., failure to provide necessary medical or mental health treatment)
- Educational (e.g., failure to educate a child or attend to special education needs)
- Emotional (e.g., inattention to a child's emotional needs, failure to provide psychological care, or permitting the child to use alcohol or other drugs

- These situations do not always mean a child is neglected. Sometimes cultural values, the standards of care in the community, and poverty may be contributing factors, indicating the family is in need of information or assistance. When a family fails to use information and resources, and the child's health or safety is at risk, then child welfare intervention may be required. In addition, many States provide an exception to the definition of neglect for parents who choose not to seek medical care for their children due to religious beliefs that may prohibit medical intervention.

Sexual abuse includes activities by a parent or caregiver such as fondling a child's genitals, penetration, incest, rape, sodomy, indecent exposure, and exploitation through prostitution or the production of pornographic materials.

Sexual abuse is defined by CAPTA as "the employment, use, persuasion, inducement, enticement, or coercion of any child to engage in, or assist any other person to engage in, any sexually explicit conduct or simulation of such conduct for the purpose of producing a visual depiction of such conduct; or the rape, and in cases of caretaker or inter-familial relationships, statutory rape, molestation, prostitution, or other form of sexual exploitation of children, or incest with children."

Emotional abuse (or psychological abuse) is a pattern of behavior that impairs a child's emotional development or sense of self-worth. This may include constant criticism, threats, or rejection, as well as withholding love, support, or guidance. Emotional abuse is often difficult to prove and, therefore, child protective services may not be able to intervene without evidence of harm or mental injury to the child. Emotional abuse is almost always present when other forms are identified.

Abandonment is now defined in many States as a form of neglect. In general, a child is considered to be abandoned when the parent's identity or whereabouts are unknown, the child has been left alone in circumstances where the child suffers serious harm, or the parent has failed to maintain contact with the child or provide reasonable support for a specified period of time.

Substance abuse is an element of the definition of child abuse or neglect in many States.[5] Circumstances that are considered abuse or neglect in some States include:

- Prenatal exposure of a child to harm due to the mother's use of an illegal drug or other substance

- Manufacture of methamphetamine in the presence of a child
- Selling, distributing, or giving illegal drugs or alcohol to a child
- Use of a controlled substance by a caregiver that impairs the caregiver's ability to adequately care for the child https://www.childwelfare.gov/pubs/factsheets/whatiscan.cfm

What Is Child Abuse and Neglect?
Legislative Analyst's Office, January 1996

http://www.lao.ca.gov/1996/010596_child_abuse/cw11096a.html#A2

Definitions and Types of Child Abuse/Neglect

State law defines child abuse as (1) physical injury inflicted on a child by another person, (2) sexual abuse, or (3) emotional abuse. Child neglect is defined as negligent treatment which threatens the child's health or welfare. The different types of child abuse/neglect can be categorized as follows:

- **Sexual abuse** is the victimization of a child by sexual activities, including molestation, indecent exposure, fondling, rape, and incest.
- **Physical abuse** is bodily injury inflicted by other than accidental means on a child, including willful cruelty, unjustifiable punishment, or corporal punishment.

8

Keeping our Children Safe from sexual predators

- **Emotional abuse** is nonphysical mistreatment, resulting in disturbed behavior by the child, such as severe withdrawal or hyperactivity. Emotional abuse includes willfully causing any child to suffer, inflicting mental suffering, or endangering a child's emotional well-being.
- **General neglect** is the negligent failure of a parent/guardian or caretaker to provide adequate food, clothing, shelter, or supervision where no physical injury to the child has occurred.
- **Severe neglect** refers to those situations of neglect where the child's health is endangered, including severe malnutrition.
- **Exploitation** means forcing or coercing a child into performing activities that are beyond the child's capabilities or which are illegal or degrading, including sexual exploitation.

Child Abuse: Physical, Sexual, Emotional, Severe Neglect

We need to know the cold heart facts regarding who abuse our children.

1. Parents/grandparents, family relatives
2. Teachers, Educators
3. Church leaders-pastors, priests, youth pastors
4. Coaches in all fields of sports.
5. Neighbors, and friends
6. Baby sitters and caregivers

7. Registered sex offenders abuse children
8. Un-registered sex offenders abuse children

Child Maltreatment 2011: Specifically, a perpetrator is the person who is responsible for the abuse or neglect of a child. 50 states reported case level data about perpetrators using unique identifiers. In these states, the total duplicated count of perpetrators was 885,003 and the total unique count or perpetrators was 508,849 for 2011.

- 4/5 (84.6%) of unique perpetrators were between the ages of 20 and 49 years.
- More than ½ (53.6%) of perpetrators were women, 45.1 % of perpetrators were men, and 1.3% were of unknown sex
- 4/5 (80.8) of duplicated perpetrators were parents
- Of the duplicated perpetrators who were parents, 87.6% were the biological parents.

Keeping our Children Safe from sexual predators

How many children died from abuse or neglect?

Child fatalities are the most tragic consequence for maltreatment. For FFY 2011, 51 states reported a total of 1,545 fatalities.

Characterics of Abuse

1. A child may appear to be different from other children in emotional or physical makeup. In some cases, parents of this child may describe him or her as being "different" or even "bad."
2. A child may seem overly fearful of his or her own parents. The child may be hesitant to go to the parent and expresses his or her fear through the hesitancy.
3. A child has extremes in behavior such as crying too easily or being overly sensitive. Or the child may block his or her emotions and appear not to care.
4. A neglected child will show evidence of poor overall care. Clothes may be dirty, torn or not fit well. In the winter, the child may not be wearing proper clothing.
5. A child may be cautious or wary of physical contact, especially with interacting with an adult. There also may be the other extreme, when an abused child appears starved for adult affection, but his or her methods or getting it are inappropriate.

6. Some children show a radical change in their general overall behavior.
7. Untrusting: Most abused children have difficulty trusting others. Treatment involves play therapy in a safe environment

Symptoms of Abused Children

- Take the Blame: Many feel they are the blame. They learn to suffer in silent. May feel unwanted.
- Feeling Anger and Rage: Children learn both to deny and to repress fear, anger, bitterness and hatred. They become hostile, defiant and the tension begins to eat away at the child.
- To empower children not to scare them
- Teach Families to become familiar with Megan's Law website: www.meganslaw.gov.ca and/or other child safety sites to help learn better ways to protect children from Sexual Predators/Registered Sex Offenders.

What is Child Victimization

There are a wide variety of forms of sexual victimization such as sexual abuse of children, sexual exploitation of children, and sexual assault of children and sexual abduction of children.

Keeping our Children Safe from sexual predators

What is Child Sexual Exploitation

This term maybe difficult to define-could mean different things to different children. It implies sexual victimization of a child perpetrated by some one other than a family member or legal guardian. It includes victimization involving sex rings, child pornography, and the use of computers, sex tourism, and child prostitution.

Missing & Exploited Children
- Every 40 seconds a Child goes missing
- More than 2,000 children goes missing a day
- More than 800,000 every year
- Another estimated 500,000 disappear without being reported
  Source: NCMEC
- 1 in 7 teenagers in the USA run away from home.
- Living on the streets, one out of every three teens will be lured into prostitution within 48 hours of leaving home.
- And the longer they are gone, the more likely they are to engage in "survival sex."
- After three months away from home, 90 percent of children will turn to sex. (National Incidence Studies of Missing, Runaway and Throwaway Children)

Sexual Assaults against Children
- One-Assault by a Child Molester can result in Multiple Victims within the family.

Keeping our Children Safe from sexual predators

- The Sound a Child Makes When Sexually assaulted is Often Silence.
- Three-of the Worst Crimes committed against Children are Rape, Molestation and In-Action-doing Nothing-is not the answer.

Internet Crimes Against Children

Types of Internet Victimization
1. Enticing them through online contact for the purpose of engaging them in sexual acts.
2. Using the Internet for the production, manufacture, and distribution of child pornography.
3. Using the Internet to expose youth to child pornography and encourage them to exchange pornography.
4. Enticing and exploiting children for the purpose of sexual tourism (travel with the intent to engage in sexual behavior) for commercial gain and/or personal gratification.

According to FBI reports
There are over 750,000 pedophiles on-line daily attempting to lure children into sexual acts, Child Pornography-exchange child pornography, child prostitution and sexual tourism-travel with intent to engage in sexual behavior.

Human Child Sex Trafficking

Human Trafficking is Illegal: Say No to Modern Day Slavery: Federal laws prohibit Sex Trafficking and Trafficking in persons for forced labor and Mistreatment. New Laws provide options for Trafficking victims regardless of Immigration status. If someone is being forced to work or held against their will we can help. It is illegal to use force or threats to make someone work to pay off a debt.

Human Trafficking is the 3rd largest criminal enterprise in the world. Los Angeles County is one of the largest trafficking ports in the United States. With the average age of entry into prostitution in the U.S. at 12-14 years old. The demand for trafficked children as sex slaves and slave labor increasing.

Preventing the sale of human beings should be an even greater priority: COV strategy to combat Human Child Trafficking: Child Safety Awareness, Education and Training.

The Trafficking Victims Protection Act of 2000 (TVPA) defines severe forms of trafficking in persons as, sex trafficking in which a commercial sex act is induced by force, fraud, or coercion, or in which the person induced to perform such act has not attained 18 years of age; or the recruitment, harboring, transportation, provision or obtaining of a person for labor or services, through the use of force, fraud or coercion for the purpose of subjection to involuntary servitude, peonage, debt bondage, or slavery (8.S.C. § 1101).

Keeping our Children Safe from sexual predators

Facts about Human Trafficking

The United States is one of the top three destination points for trafficked victims and California, New York, Texas and Nevada are the top destination states within the country.

Los Angeles is one of the top three points of entry into this country for victims of slavery and trafficking. This trafficking route occurs in a triangle from Los Angeles, California to Las Vegas, Nevada, and back to Sacramento, California. The diverse communities of these sprawling cities make it easier to hide and move victims from place to place. Which makes it very difficult for law enforcement to locate potential survivors?

Sacramento is among the top 5 cities in the United States experiencing an epidemic of child trafficking.

Immigration agents estimate that 10,000 women are being held in Los Angeles' underground brothels; this does not include the thousands of victims in domestic work, sweatshops or other informal industries.

Women who have been trafficked for the purpose of sexual exploitation experience a significantly higher rate of HIV and other STDs, tuberculosis, and permanent damage to their reproductive systems.

Trafficking victims normally don't get help because they think that they or their families will be hurt by their traffickers, or that they will be deported.

Human trafficking has been identified as the largest human-rights violation in the history of mankind.

Child Safety is everyone responsibility

"Parents, guardians, and members of the community must all work together to help ensure children will be protected and have access to help if they need it. Child safety is all our responsibilities." — Nancy McBride, NCMEC's National Safety Director

Child Safety is important to our entire community, city, state and nationwide. Most crimes against children most often result from lack of parental supervision, along with lack of the watchful eyes and ears of Community Child Safety Advocates in the neighborhood parks, schools, and communities. As a result, Sexual predators wait for the opportune time to attack, and lured our children in the community and online into their control and manipulation.

Denial

Our Children are in Crisis: Are we in Denial?
<u>COV is addressing the "Denial"</u> **How can we address the denial?**

America historical perspective of society's general attitudes about sexual victimization of children is one word "Denial." Most people do not want to hear about it and would prefer to pretend such victimization just does not happen.

However, it is difficult to pretend that it does not happen. New stores and reports about child sexual abuse and exploitation are daily occurrences. It is imperative that as Child Safety advocates, we must be ready to address this denial. Being educated, trained, informed, and trying to overcome and encourage society to address, report, and prevent the sexual victimization of children.

To help address the denial: COV is recruiting CCSA, Community Child Safety Advocates for a 6 week training (Webinar) to be the "Extra eyes and Ears) in the community reaching out to protect, educate and inform children/parents and community regarding the safety and well being of children. Upon completion: CCSA Certificate given to graduates. Courses are also provided via correspondence

Keeping our Children Safe from sexual predators

Awareness is our best defense.

- Awareness is the state or ability to perceive, to feel, or to be conscious of events, objects or sensory patterns:

- Awareness is knowing or realizing; conscious; informed; having knowledge of; being vigilant, watchful; raise/increase awareness of; increased/heightened awareness; relating to increasing people's awareness; the ability to notice things

- Awareness is our best defense. Be in the Know! Be informed and work to prevent Child Victimization. Learn better ways to defend, and protect children from sexual predators in community and online; in addition to Missing and exploited Children and Child Human Trafficking by being the extra eyes and ears in your communities.

Child Safety Education and Training

COV Statistical FACT SHEET:

There is an Epidemic our children are facing regarding their safety and well being.

- A National Crisis: The exposure of America's children to violence as victims and as witnesses. (Attorney Eric Holder, DOJ)

- Children's exposure to violence, whether as victims or witnesses, is often associated with long-term physical, psychological and emotional harm. Children exposed to violence are also at a higher risk of engaging in criminal behavior later in life and becoming part of a cycle of violence. (DOJ, Assistant Attorney General Tom Perrelli)

- To develop Child Safety knowledge and raise a high level of community awareness that will ultimately improve homes, cities, towns and communities.
- Solution: To increase Community Awareness in protecting children from sexual predators.

- COV commitment is to provide community-grass root support, parental training, child safety education and child safety literature to families in community.

- Develop and maintain collaborative partnerships with County, City, State and Law Enforcement Agencies.

- Goals: To help prevent children's exposure to sexual assaults; to mitigate the negative impact of children's exposure to sexual assaults; to develop knowledge and spread awareness about children's exposure to sexual assaults; to reduce child victimization and learn better ways to protect and keep our children safe from sexual predators in the community; to Promote Community Awareness regarding Child Safety: Press Release, Newsletters, PSA, Child Safety News Reports via Radio, Television and Cable Television.

- Recruit and Train (12) Child Safety Advocates in each community where Workshops are held. Certificates awarded at the end of 6 weeks training.
- Community Partnerships: LAPD, LA County Sheriff Department, California DOJ (Department of Justice), Center for Missing and Exploited Children, Los Angeles District Attorney's Office, Los Angeles Probation Department, and many other Local agencies.

- Child Safety education and training should be top priority due to the need for a concerted effort to reduce persistently greater violent crimes against children in addition to sex crimes against children and injuries among high-risk populations.

- We must not understate the existing child safety situation, however. There are real child safety risks that must be reduced.

Keeping our Children Safe from sexual predators

- While there are many quick and relatively direct solutions that are in progress, major community Child Safety Workshops is a continuous process that never ends.

Source: www.doj.gov

Child Safety Quotes to live by

"The only thing necessary for the triumph of evil is for good people to do nothing." Edmund Burke

"Throughout the US, girls are being bought and sold to adults. Girls are sold on the streets, in strip clubs, brothels, truck stops, and with increasing frequency on internet sites like Craigslist and Back page." Rachel Lloyd, Founder & Executive Director, GEM.

According to, Office of Victims & Crimes, OVC (Director, John W. Gillis), "Children have always been vulnerable to victimization. Their trusting natures and naïveté make them perfect targets for perpetrators—both people they know and those they don't. As children grow into adolescents, they remain vulnerable to victimization."

"It's an unfortunate fact of life that pedophiles are everywhere online" said Special Agent Greg Wing, who supervises a cyber squad in our Chicago Field Office.

Keeping our Children Safe from sexual predators

"Protecting our children is our solemn responsibility. It's what we must do. When a child's life or innocence is taken it is a terrible loss -- it's an act of unforgivable cruelty. Our society has a duty to protect our children from exploitation and danger."

-President George W. Bush

Keeping our Children Safe from sexual predators

Our Children are valuable and special.

It is all of our responsibility to protect them

Our children

Our children are valuable and special. They are the weakest members of our society. The most vulnerable ones, who look up to parents, caregivers, teachers and authority figures to teach, educate, inform and guide them in a loving, caring and safe environment. We must protect them from dangers and potential risks of sexual predators in the community as well as, on-line. MC Campbell

According to, Office of Victims & Crimes, OVC (Director, John W. Gillis), "Children have always been vulnerable to victimization. Their trusting natures and naïveté make them perfect targets for perpetrators—both people they know and those they don't. As children grow into adolescents, they remain vulnerable to victimization."

Keeping our Children Safe from sexual predators

U.S. Department of Justice (DOJ) Fast Facts

1. Children exposed to violence are more likely to abuse drugs and alcohol; suffer from depression, anxiety, and post-traumatic disorders;

2. Children fail or have difficulty in school; and become delinquent and engage in criminal behavior when victim of violence.

3. 60% of American children were exposed to violence, crime, or abuse in their homes, schools, and communities

4. Almost 40% of American children were direct victims of 2 or more violent acts, and 1 and 10 were victims of violence 5 or more times.

5. Children are more likely to be exposed to violence and crime than adults

6. Almost 1 in 10 American children saw one family member assault another family member, and more than 25% had been exposed to family violence during their life.

7. A child's exposure to one type of violence increases the likelihood that the child will be exposed to other types of violence and exposed multiple times.

Keeping our Children Safe from sexual predators

Reference:

Defending Childhood Initiative
Finkelhor, D., Turner, H. Ormrod, R., Hamby, S., and Kracke, K. 2009. Children's Exposure to Violence: A Comprehensive National Survey. Bulletin. Washington, DC: U.S. Department of Justice. Office of Justice, Office of Juvenile Justice and Delinquency Prevention. More Information is available at www.ncjrs.gov/pdffiles1/ojidp/227744.pdf. or www.unh.edu/ccrc/projects/natscev.html.

Keeping our Children Safe from sexual predators

Contents

Keeping our Children Safe from sexual predators

Chapter I *__Missing and Exploited Children__*

Did you know?

1. Every 40 seconds a child goes missing
2. More than 2,000 a day child goes missing
3. More than 800,000 every year.
4. Another estimated-500,000 disappear without being reported
5. For the most part, these bodies are never found. (NCMEC)

A Need to Know:

- 1-7 teens in the US run away from home.
- Living on the streets, one out of every three teens will be lured into prostitution within 48 hours of leaving home.
- And the longer they are gone, the more likely they are to engage in "survival sex."
- After 3 months away from home, 90% of children will turn to sex. (National Incidence Studies of Missing, Runaway and Thrownaway Children)

The problem of missing children is complex and multifaceted. There are different types of missing children including *family abductions*; *endangered runaways*; *non-family abductions*; and *lost, injured, or otherwise missing* children. When the public hears of a missing child case, it is generally involving one of the estimated 115 child victims of the most serious, long-term non-family abduction called "stereotypical kidnappings".

Keeping our Children Safe from sexual predators

Non family abduction

Non family abduction occurs when a non family perpetrator takes a child by the use of physical force or threat of bodily harm or detain a child for at least 1 hour in an isolated place by the use of physical force or threat of bodily harm without lawful authority or parental permission; or when a child who is younger than 15 years old or is mentally incompetent, without lawful authority or parental permission, is taken or detained by or voluntarily accompanies a non family perpetrator who conceals the child's whereabouts, demands ransom, or expresses the intention to keep the child permanently.

Stereotypical Kidnapping

Stereotypical Kidnapping occurs when a stranger or slight acquaintance perpetrates a non family abduction in which the child is detained overnight, transported at least 50 miles, held for ransom, abducted with intent to keep the child permanently, or killed.

Family Abduction

A family abduction occurs when, in violation of a custody order, a decree, or other legitimate custodial rights, a member of the child's family, or someone acting on behalf of a family member, takes or fails to return a child, and the child is concealed or transported out of State with the intent to prevent contact or deprive the caretaker of custodial rights indefinitely or permanently. For a child or older, unless mentally incompetent, there must be evidence that the perpetrator used physical force or threat of bodily harm to take or detain the child.

Runaway/Thrownaway

A runaway incident occurs when a child leaves home without permission and stays away overnight, or a child 14 years old or younger for older and mentally incompetent who is away from home chooses not to return when supposed to and stays away overnight, or a child 15 years old or older who is away from home chooses not to return and stays away 2 night.

A thrownaway incident occurs when a child is asked or told to leave home by a parent or other household adult, no adequate alternative care is arranged for the child by a household adult, and the child is out of the household overnight, of a child who is away from home is prevented from returning home by a parent or other household adult, no adequate alternative care is arranged for the child by a household adult, and the child Is out of the household overnight.

Missing Involuntary, Lost, or Injured

A missing involuntary, lost, or injured episode occurs when a child's whereabouts are unknown to the child's caretaker and this causes the caretaker to be alarmed for at least 1 hour and try to locate the child, under one of two conditions (1) the child was trying to get home or make contact with the caretaker but was unable to do so because the child was lost , stranded, or injured, or (2) the child was too young to know how to return home or make contact with the caretaker.

- Missing Benign Explanation
- A missing benign explanation episode occurs when a child's whereabouts are unknown to the child's caretaker and this causes the caretaker to (1) be alarmed, (2) try to locate the child, and (3) contact the police about the episode for any reason, as long as the child was not lost, injured abducted, victimized, or classified as runaway/thrownaway.

Missing involuntary, lost, or injured events.

Ref: The first National Incidence Studies of Missing, Abducted, Runaway, and Thrownaway Children (NISMART, October 2002, National Estimates of Missing Children: An Overview)

Washington, DC: Office of Juvenile Justice and Delinquency Prevention, Office of Justice Programs, U.S. Department of Justice, October 2002, page 5. www.ojjdp.ncjrs.org

Keeping our Children Safe from sexual predators

Act immediately if your Child is missing

- If your child is missing from home, search the house, checking closets, piles of laundry, in and under beds, inside large appliances, and inside vehicles, including trunks-wherever a child may crawl or hide.
- If you still cannot find your child ACT IMMEDIATELY call your local law enforcement agency.
- If your child disappears in a store, notify the store manager or security office. Then immediately call your local law enforcement agency.
- Many stores have a Code Adam plan of action-if a child is missing in the store, employees immediately mobilize to look for the missing child.
- When you call law enforcement, provide your child's name, date of birth, height, weight, and any other unique identifiers such as eyeglasses and braces. Tell them what you notices that your child was missing and what clothing he or she was wearing.
- Request that your child's name and identifying information be immediately entered into the National Crime Information Center (NCIC) Missing Person File.
- After you have reported your child missing to law enforcement, call the National Center for Missing & Exploited

Keeping our Children Safe from sexual predators

Children (NCMEC) on our toll-free telephone number: 1-800-THE-LOST (1-800-843-5678). Ref. NCMEC

- For support and guidance, you can contact Los Angeles, Children of Victory, 323-464-5431

Child Safety Tips

What are the most important things parents should tell children about safety?

1. Always check first with a parent, guardian, or trusted adult before going anywhere, accepting anything, or getting into a car with anyone.
2. Do not go out alone. Always take a friend with when going places or playing outside.
3. Say no if someone tries to touch you, or treats you in a way that makes you feel sad, scared, or confused. Get out of the situation as quickly as possible.
4. Tell a parent, guardian, or trusted adult if you feel sad, scared, or confused.
5. There will always be someone to help you, and you have the right to be safe.

What should a parent know when talking to a child about safety?

1. Don't forget your older children. Children aged 11 to17 are equally at risk to victimization. At the same time you are giving your older children more freedom,

Keeping our Children Safe from sexual predators

make sure they understand important safety rules as well.

2. Speak to your children in a manner that is calm and reassuring. Children do not need to be frightened to get the point across. In fact, fear can thwart the safety message, because fear can be paralyzing to a child.

3. Speak openly. Children will be less likely to come to you about issues enshrouded in secrecy. If they feel that you are comfortable discussing the subject at hand, they may be more forthcoming.

4. Do not teach "stranger danger." Children do not have the same understanding of "strangers" as adults; the concept is difficult for them to grasp. And, based on what we know about those who harm children, people known to children and/or their families' actually present greater danger to children than do "strangers."

5. Practice what you preach. You may think your children understand your message, but until they can incorporate it into their daily lives, it may not be clearly understood. Find opportunities to practice "what if" scenarios.

6. Teach your children that safety is more important than manners. In other words, it is more important for children to get themselves out of a dangerous situation than it is to be polite. They also need to know that it is okay to tell you what happened, and they won't be tattletales.

Keeping our Children Safe from sexual predators

Is "stranger danger"—that dangers to kids come from strangers—really a myth?
Yes. In the majority of cases, the perpetrator is someone the parents or child knows, and that person may be in a position of trust or responsibility to the child and family.

We have learned that children do not have the same understanding of who a stranger is as an adult might, therefore, it is a difficult concept for the child to grasp. It is much more beneficial to children to help them build the confidence and self-esteem they need to stay as safe as possible in any potentially dangerous situation they encounter rather than teaching them to be "on the look out" for a particular type of person.

For decades, parents, guardians, and teachers have told children to "stay away from strangers" in an effort to keep them safe. In response to the on-going debate about the effectiveness of such programs, NCMEC released the research-based Guidelines for Programs to Reduce Child Victimization: A

Resource for Communities When Choosing a Program to Teach Personal Safety to Children to assist schools as they select curricula aimed at reducing crimes against children.

For more information on child safety, please visit the More Publications section of this website. Pay particular attention to Child Safety Is More Than a Slogan; Child Protection; and Guidelines for Programs to Reduce Child

Keeping our Children Safe from sexual predators

Victimization: A Resource for Communities When Choosing a Program to Teach Personal Safety to Children

What other advice can you offer parents about talking to kids?
Parents should choose opportunities or "teachable" moments to reinforce safety skills. If an incident occurs in your community and your child asks you about it, speak frankly but with reassurance.

Explain to your children that you want to discuss the safety rules with them, so that they will know what to do if they are ever confronted with a potentially dangerous situation. Make sure you have "safety nets" in place, so that our children know there is always someone who can help them.
What child safety education resources does the National Center for Missing & Exploited Children provide?

The National Center for Missing & Exploited Children offers a wealth of resources to help educate parents, children, law enforcement, and the general public about child safety.

[Safety tips adapted from Know the Rules...General Parental Tips to Help Keep Your Children Safer. Copyright© 2000 National Center for Missing & Exploited Children (NCMEC). All rights reserved.]

Keeping our Children Safe from sexual predators

Understanding of Consumers:
Consumers need to understand that the first line of defense for families is safety education and line-of-sight supervision of their children. If a device is to be used, understand what it can do and cannot do, that machines can fail, and that the tracking device should be, if they choose, an element within a complete safety program for their family. Ref. NCMEC

Additional Information on keeping our children safe.

What kinds of things can I do to keep the children in my life safer?

There is no substitute for your attention and supervision. Being available and taking time to know and listen to your children helps build feelings of safety and security. Here are some tips and suggestions to help empower your children and you.

- Listen to your children
- Take the time to talk to your children
- Know who your children's friends are
- Notice when anyone shows one or all of your children too much attention or begins giving them gifts
- Teach your children that they should say NO to any unwelcome, uncomfortable, or confusing touches or actions by others
- Be sensitive to any changes in your children's behavior or attitude

Keeping our Children Safe from sexual predators

- Look and listen to small clues that something may be troubling your children because children are not always comfortable disclosing disturbing events or feelings
- If your children do share problems with you, strive to remain calm, noncritical, and nonjudgmental
- Be sure to screen babysitters and caregivers
- Provide oversight and supervision of your children's online computer use
- Be involved in your children's activities
- Work with your children's school to institute sound child-safety programs as part of their curriculum
- Practice basic safety skills with your children, and discuss their safety openly and honestly

[1]As reported by Andrea J. Sedlak, David Finkelhor, Heather Hammer, and Dana J. Schultz, "National Estimates of Missing Children: An Overview," *National Incidence Studies of Missing, Abducted, Runaway, and Thrownaway Children,* Washington, DC: Office of Juvenile Justice and Delinquency Prevention, Office of Justice Programs, U.S. Department of Justice, October 2002, page 5, an estimated 797,500 children were reported missing in 1999. An NCMEC review of the Federal Bureau of Investigations National Crime Information Center missing-person reports shows a range of entries from 818,921 to 929,518 for the past 6 years. Traditionally 80% of these entries are for people younger

than 18.
[2]David Finkelhor. "Current information on the Scope and Nature of Child Sexual Abuse." *The Future of Children: Sexual Abuse of Children,* 1994, Volume 4, page 37.

How can I prepare myself in case my child becomes missing?

1. Keep a complete description of your child on hand
2. Take color photographs of your child every six months
3. Have your dentist prepare and maintain dental charts for your child, and be sure they are updated each time an examination or dental work is performed
4. Know where your child's medical records are located
5. Arrange with your local law-enforcement agency to have your child fingerprinted and keep the fingerprints in a safe and easily accessible place
6. Keep a DNA sample from your child, like an old toothbrush in a brown envelope licked closed by your child, at room temperature in a dry, easily accessible place that is far away from heat

What should I do if my child is missing?

1. The most important thing to remember is to act immediately. If a murder is to be committed it typically happens within the first 3 hours after abduction.[3]

2. Search your home and check with relatives, neighbors, and friends to try and locate your child.
3. If you cannot find your child, immediately report your child missing to your local law-enforcement officers.
4. Limit access to your home until law-enforcement officers arrive and are able to collect evidence. Give law-enforcement officers all the information they request about your child, and be sure to give them any information that could help in the search. Request that your child's name and identifying information be immediately entered into the National Crime Information Center (NCIC) Missing Person File.
5. Call the National Center for Missing & Exploited Children (NCMEC) at 1-800-THE-LOST® (1-800-843-5678) to find out what resources are available to you.

[3]Katherine M. Brown, Robert D. Keppel, Joseph G. Weis, and Marvin E. Skeen. *CASE MANAGEMENT for Missing Children Homicide Investigation*. Olympia, Washington: Office of the Attorney General, State of Washington, and U.S. Department of Justice's Office of Juvenile Justice and Delinquency Prevention, May 2006, page 13.

These guidelines are adapted from the brochures titled *Just in Case...Parental guidelines in case your child might someday be missing, Just in Case...Parental guidelines in case your child might someday be the victim of sexual exploitation*, and *Preventing the Sexual*

Keeping our Children Safe from sexual predators

Exploitation of Children. Copyright © respectively 1985, 1985, and 2003 National Center for Missing & Exploited Children. All rights reserved.

A Partial List of some of the early reports of **Missing Children:**

- Ethan Patz: 1972
- Atlanta Missing Children: 1975
- Adam Walsh 1975

Etan Kalil Patz; October 9, 1972 - declared legally dead in 2001) was an American child who was six years old when he disappeared in Lower Manhattan, New York City, on May 25, 1979.- He is arguably the most famous missing child of New York City. His disappearance helped spark the missing children's movement, including new legislation and various methods for tracking down missing children, such as the milk carton campaigns of the mid-1980s. Etan was the first ever missing child to be pictured on the side of a milk carton.

The **Atlanta Child Murders**, known locally as the "missing and murdered children case", were a series of murders committed in Atlanta, Georgia, United States from the summer of 1979 until the spring of 1981. Over the two-year period, a minimum of 28 African-American children, adolescents and adults were killed. Atlanta native Wayne Williams, also African American and 23-years-old at the time of the last murder, was arrested for and convicted of two of the murders.

Keeping our Children Safe from sexual predators

Adam John Walsh

Adam John Walsh

(November 14, 1974 – July 27, 1981) was an American boy who was abducted from a Sears department store at the Hollywood Mall in Hollywood, Florida, on July 27, 1981, and later found murdered and decapitated. Walsh's death earned national publicity. His story was made into the 1983 television film *Adam*, seen by 38 million people in its original airing. Walsh's father, John Walsh, became an advocate for victims of violent crimes and the host of the television program *America's Most Wanted*.

Child Abduction Emergency History: They were innocent children who lives were destroyed by predators. We need to know their story.

1. Amber Hagerman: Texas:1996
2. Levi Frady: Georgia: 1997
3. Morgan Nick: Arkansas: 1995
4. Maile Gilbert: Hawaii: 1985
5. Megan Kanka: New Jersey: 1994
6. Jacob Wetterling: Minnesota: 1989

Keeping our Children Safe from sexual predators

AMBER ALERT

An AMBER Alert or a Child Abduction Emergency (SAME code: CAE) is a child abduction alert bulletin in several countries throughout the world, issued upon the suspected abduction of a child, since 1996. AMBER is officially a acronym for "America's Missing: Broadcasting Emergency Response" but was originally named for Amber Hagerman, a 9-year-old child who was abducted and murdered in Arlington, Texas in 1996. Alternate alert names are used in Georgia, where it is called "Levi's Call"[1] (named after Levi Frady); Hawaii, where it is called a "Maile Amber Alert" (named after Maile Gilbert); and Arkansas, where it is called a "Morgan Nick Amber Alert" (in memory of Morgan Chauntel Nick). Frady, Gilbert and Nick were all children who went missing in those U.S. states.

AMBER Alerts are distributed via commercial radio stations, satellite radio, television stations, and cable TV by the Emergency Alert System and NOAA Weather Radio[1] (where they are termed "Child Abduction Emergency" or "Amber Alerts"). The alerts are also issued via e-mail, electronic traffic-condition signs, the LED billboards which are located outside of newer Walgreens locations, along with the LED/LCD signs of billboard companies such as Clear Channel Outdoor, CBS Outdoor and Lamar, or through wireless device SMS text messages.

Keeping our Children Safe from sexual predators

WHO WAS AMBER?

Amber Rene Hagerman
Born November 25, 1986
Arlington, Texas, US

Amber Rene Hagerman (November 25, 1986 – January 15, 1996) was a young girl who became a victim of an abduction and murder. On January 13, 1996, she was riding her bike near her grandparents' home in Arlington, Texas, and was kidnapped soon thereafter. Her murder would later inspire the creation of the AMBER Alert system.

Facts: On January 13, 1996, Amber was visiting her grandparents at their home in Arlington, Texas. Her grandparents kept two bicycles for Amber and her younger brother Ricky. The children asked if they could go for a quick ride, and Amber's mother and grandfather said yes but only to go around the block. Amber and Ricky pedaled around two corners, before Ricky stopped and said "I'm going back because Mama said only to go around the block", and Amber carried on riding to the parking lot of an abandoned grocery store. Neighborhood kids enjoyed riding on a ramp there, so Amber rode round a few times, within the view of Jim Kevil. According to Kevil, a white or Hispanic man in a black pickup truck sprinted up to Amber and dragged her into his truck. When Ricky got home, his grandparents and mother asked where Amber was, and he said he didn't know. They told him to go and look for her, and when he returned, he said "I can't find sissy". When Amber's grandfather drove round to the parking lot looking for Amber, the police had arrived, who told him that Kevil had seen a man kidnapping a young girl. Police rushed to the scene, but all they found was a bicycle. Amber's grandfather said "that's my granddaughter's bicycle". Amber was the second child in her family to have been kidnapped. Her father's two-day-old granddaughter was abducted in 1991 and recovered safely 10 hours later.

Arlington police began searching for Amber immediately. Volunteers searched for Amber Hagerman for several days, and the Federal Bureau of Investigation investigated. Four days after her abduction, a man walking his dog found Amber's corpse in a creek bed. An autopsy revealed that her throat had been cut. She had been alive two whole days before being killed. Although a $75,000 reward was offered for information leading to Amber's killer, he was never found. The task force investigating Amber's murder was dissolved in June 1997.

Keeping our Children Safe from sexual predators

Megan's Law: WHO WAS MEGAN?

Megan Kanka

http://www.meganslaw.ca.gov

Megan's Laws are named for Megan Kanka, a seven-year-old girl from New Jersey who was sexually assaulted and murdered in 1994 by a neighbor who, unknown to the victim's family, had been previously convicted for sex offenses against children

MEGAN'S LAW is an informal name for laws in the United States requiring law enforcement authorities to make information available to the public regarding registered sex offenders. Individual states decide what information will be made available and how it should be disseminated. Commonly included information includes the offender's name, picture, address, incarceration date, and nature of crime. The information is often displayed on free public websites, but can be published in newspapers, distributed in pamphlets, or through various other means.

Keeping our Children Safe from sexual predators

At the federal level, Megan's Law is known as the Sexual Offender (Jacob Wetterling) Act of 1994, and requires persons convicted of sex crimes against children to notify local law enforcement of any change of address or employment after release from custody (prison or psychiatric facility). The notification requirement may be imposed for a fixed period of time - usually at least ten years - or permanently.

Some states may legislate registration for all sex crimes, even if no minors were involved. It is a felony in most jurisdictions to fail to register or fail to update information.

History on Megan's Law: A must read:

Megan's Law provides two major information services to the public: sex offender registration and community notification. The details of what is provided as part of sex offender registration and how community notification is handled vary from state to state, and in some states the required registration information and community notification protocols have changed many times since Megan's Law was passed. The Adam Walsh Child Protection and Safety Act supplements Megan's Law with new registration requirements and a three-tier system for classifying sex offenders according to their risk to the community.

Megan's Laws are state and federal statutes that require convicted sex offenders to register with local police. Sex offenders are required to

Keeping our Children Safe from sexual predators

register with local police and to notify law enforcement authorities whenever they move to a new location. The statutes establish a notification process to provide information about sex offenders to law enforcement agencies and, when appropriate, to the public. The type of notification is based on an evaluation of the risk to the community from a particular offender the brutality of the crimes in the Megan Kanka case provided the impetus for laws that mandate registration of sex offenders and corresponding community notification. In 1994, Congress passed the Jacob Wetterling Crimes Against Children and Sexually Violent Offender Registration Act, Title 17, 108 Stat.2038, as amended, 42 U.S.C. § 14071. This precursor to a federal Megan's Law conditioned certain federal law enforcement funds on state adoption of sex offender registration laws and set minimum standards for state programs. By 1996, every State, the District of Columbia, and the Federal Government had enacted some variation of Megan's Law.

Under the federal Megan's Law statute, states have discretion to establish criteria for disclosure, but they must make private and personal information on registered sex offenders available to the public. The premise of Megan's Law is that communities will be better able to protect their children if they are informed of the descriptions and whereabouts of high-risk sex offenders. Notification of sex-offender information to the community assists law enforcement in investigations, provides legal grounds to detain known sex offenders, may deter sex offenders from committing new offenses, and offers citizens information that they can use to protect their children.

Megan's Laws were not created without controversy. Opponents argue that the statutes encourage acts of vigilantism and do not give offenders who have paid their dues the chance to merge back into society. But actions taken against the convicted sex offender, including vandalism of property, verbal or written threats, or actual physical violence against the offender, their family, or employer, could lead to arrest and prosecution for criminal acts. Despite these concerns, however, federal and state legislatures have continued to reinforce and broaden the scope of these statutes.

On May 17, 1996, federal efforts to strengthen the Jacob Wetterling Act got a boost when President Bill Clinton signed an amendment to the violent crime control and law enforcement act of 1994 (42 U.S.C. 14071); the amendment is known as Megan's Law. This legislation directs all state legislatures to adopt laws requiring convicted sex offenders to register with their local law enforcement agency after release. Additionally, the federal Megan's Law mandates states to grant access to sex-offender registries to the public. Although sex-offender registration for law enforcement purposes had been required previously, the idea of community notification was relatively new.

Keeping our Children Safe from sexual predators

The legislation has undergone many adaptations in the states. While the details of state Megan's Laws differ from jurisdiction to jurisdiction, conviction of any one or more of the following offenses will require convicts to register pursuant to Megan's Laws:

- aggravated sexual assault,
- sexual assault,
- aggravated criminal sexual contact,
- endangering the welfare of a child by engaging in sexual conduct that would impair or debauch the morals of the child,
- luring or enticing,
- kidnapping (if the victim is a minor and the offender not a parent),
- criminal restraint, and
- False imprisonment.

Megan's Laws have guidelines that list factors law that enforcement agencies are to consider when weighing the risk of re-offense. These include some or all of the following:

- post-incarceration supervision,
- the status of therapy or counseling,
- criminal background,
- degree of remorse for criminal acts,
- substance abuse,
- employment or schooling status,
- psychological or psychiatric profile, and
- Any history of threats or of stalking locations where children congregate.

Keeping our Children Safe from sexual predators

State sex offender registries include sex offenders' names, descriptions and photographs, addresses, places of employment or school (if applicable), descriptions of the offenders' vehicles and license plate numbers, and brief descriptions of the offenses for which the sex offender was convicted.

Prosecutors and courts are responsible for determining who should receive direct notice of the presence of a particular individual in a community.

In 2003, 39 states provided access to sex offender information in searchable databases on the Internet. Arkansas, California, Colorado, Hawaii, Idaho, Maine, Maryland, Massachusetts, Nevada, Rhode Island, and Vermont either did not provide Internet access or restricted access. Various law enforcement agencies and some private citizens or civic groups also publish listings that are specific to counties or communities. Most, if not all, of these sites are freely available regardless of the residence of the individual who is searching for information.

As with the state laws themselves, state sex offender databases have little or no uniformity. Some, like those for Alaska, Connecticut, and Florida, include photographs, physical descriptions, dates of birth, and details concerning the offenses for which offenders were convicted. The Virginia sex-offender list stores home and work addresses, while

Keeping our Children Safe from sexual predators

Indiana's contains only the city where the sex offender resides.

Most of the databases permit searching by zip code or name. Kansas allows searching by partial zip codes, while Alaska and Delaware allow searching by street name or by partial address, and Indiana permits searching by Social Security number.

While Megan's Laws do provide some measure of increased security for some parents and individuals who are concerned about the likelihood of convicted sex offenders in their midst, they cannot guarantee the public's protection from offenders who are determined to re-offend. The statutes cannot even guarantee absolute accuracy of the information contained on their registries. While offenders must register with the local police upon release from prison, many give incomplete or even false details. Others have given their details, but have traveled to areas where no one has been warned about them for the purposes of committing additional sex offenses. Critics of the measures point out that only 80 percent of pedophiles comply with registration requirements in the US, as compared with 97 percent in the United Kingdom. They also note that most cases of child abuse occur within the family, and suggest that victims might stay silent if they know that a family member will be prosecuted. But in spite of these arguments, Megan's Laws receive widespread support in communities and legislatures.

Keeping our Children Safe from sexual predators

In addition to compliance and enforcement problems with Megan's Laws, privacy advocates have challenged existing public-records laws that allow the availability of personal data via websites. In 2003, the U.S. Supreme Court handed down major decisions upholding the constitutionality of Megan's Laws. The Court upheld Connecticut's Megan's Law by a vote of 9 to 0 and upheld Alaska's legislation in a 6-to-3 decision.

In *Connecticut Dept. of Public Safety v. Doe*, 123 S. Ct. 1160, 155 L. Ed. 2d 98, 71 USLW 4125, 71 USLW 4158, 3 Cal. Daily Op. Serv. 1957, 2003 Daily Journal D.A.R. 2471, 16 Fla. L. Weekly Fed. S 140 (2003). Connecticut's Megan's Law was challenged by a convicted sex offender, John Doe. Doe protested that the Internet listing violated his due process rights because he was never given a hearing to disprove the suggestion that he might represent a continuing danger to the community. A federal judge and a three-judge federal appeals court panel agreed with Doe, striking down the law. But the Supreme Court overturned those decisions, stating that the key factor causing sex offenders to be listed in Connecticut's Internet registry is a prior conviction for a sex offense, not whether an individual might present a continued danger to the community.

The court said that statutes such as Connecticut's Megan's Law provide an important service that helps to protect society from those who would prey on its weakest

Keeping our Children Safe from sexual predators

members. Even though Megan's Laws create certain burdens for sex offenders, the court wrote that such laws do not amount to a form of ex post facto punishment, nor do they violate the Constitution's due process requirements.

In the Alaska case, *Smith v. Doe*, 123 S. Ct. 1140, 155 L. Ed. 2d 164, 71 USLW 4125, 71 USLW 4182, 3 Cal. Daily Op. Serv. 1974, 2003 Daily Journal D.A.R. 2474, 16 Fla. L. Weekly Fed. S. 142 (2003) (No. 01-729). Alaska's Megan's Law was challenged by two convicted sex offenders who already had served their prison sentences prior to passage of that state's version of the law. The two men, John Doe I and John Doe II, argued that the law was another form of punishment imposed after they already had completed their punishment. They claimed that the law failed to recognize the possibility that they might be rehabilitated and that they might no longer pose a danger to others. In previous litigation, a federal judge found no ex post facto violation, but an appeals court panel reversed, striking down the law.

The high court wrote that Alaska's Megan's Law is a civil, non-punitive regulatory effort to account for the whereabouts of convicted sex offenders. Writing for the majority, Justice Kennedy stated that there was nothing in the statute to suggest that the legislature intended to create anything other than a civil scheme designed to protect the public from harm. And even though the law applied to sex offenders who already had been released from prison, it was not an extra form of punishment.

Keeping our Children Safe from sexual predators

In these two cases, the U.S. Supreme Court effectively disposed of the principal legal arguments against Megan's Laws. In short, the Court found that state laws that are designed to use the Internet to notify parents of the presence of convicted rapists and child molesters in their own neighborhoods do not violate the constitutional rights of the listed sex offenders.
(http://lawbrain.com/wiki/Megan's_Law).

On April 20, 2009, a group of college students with Bauder College's Cold Case Investigative Research Institute began a year-long pursuit to solve the case. The volunteers have also reviewed other high-profile cold-cases such as Chandra Levy.[6]

Latest News Report on Amber's case: WFAA
Posted on March 7, 2011 at 11:00 PM
Updated Tuesday, Mar 8 at 7:59 PM

ARLINGTON — It's a criminal case that reverberated across America 15 years ago: Amber Hagerman was kidnapped while riding her bike. The 10-year-old's body was found in an Arlington creek four days later. Her throat had been slashed.

Amber's killer never found, and after all these years, detectives are still assigned to the case. Now police confirm are working a new lead following a child pornography bust in a small Texas town. While thousands of leads in the Amber Hagerman case have come and gone, these days investigators get about six tips a

Keeping our Children Safe from sexual predators

year — including a recent one from police in Ennis, where investigators arrested Sharon and Buddy Anderson for allegedly creating child pornography.

"We've got close to 200 VHS tapes," said Ennis police Sgt. Mark Mahoney. The videos and photos show graphic images of small children and were discovered inside the Andersons' Ennis apartment. At the same time, investigators also stumbled across a new witness who is now working with Arlington Police. "We're just feeding them the information," Mahoney said. "Hopefully something we're giving them will help." Neither police department is discussing the exact nature of the evidence, but Ennis investigators confirm they've contacted police in Arizona, trying to reach a man who used to work in Arlington in the mid 90s.

Amber's mother, Donna Norris, just learned the news over the last few days. "If you get too excited and too hopeful, it's a lot harder to bring yourself down from that," she said. This has been a true test of patience for her family — balancing their sorrow with hope for new leads in the unsolved case with a renewed sense of hope that her killer can be brought to justice.

"My daughter fought for her life," Norris said. "I knew she was a hard fighter then, and I'm not going to give up on her. I love her to death; she's my baby; I'll never give up hope — never." And neither will police.

Keeping our Children Safe from sexual predators

Arlington still has a detective assigned to the Amber Hagerman case, and we're told he is the one working on this intriguing new lead.

CASE Solved: HAWAII AMBERT ALERT: Maile Gilbert: THE MAILE ALERT:

Maile Gilbert

Maile, 6, was abducted from her home in Kailua, Hawaii, during a family party on August 25, 1985. She was raped, sodomized, chocked and drowned afterwards and her body was found the next day in a shallow grave along the shoreline, between Mokuleia and Kaena Point on the northwest corner of Oahu, Hawaii. James Lounsbery from Ka'a'awa, an acquaintance of Maile's father, was convicted of murdering her. He is serving a life sentence in prison. Maile was a first-grader at Aikahi Elementary School when she died. The MAILE Alert, Hawaii's equivalent of an Amber Alert, was named after her. The MAILE Alert notifies the public of abducted children through radio and television bulletins and electronic highway billboards. All bio information is from the website Children Who Never Made It Home

Keeping our Children Safe from sexual predators

Levi Frady Call <u>Unsolved:</u>

Levi Frady

Levi Frady (March 6, 1986 - October 22, 1997) was a kidnapping victim in Georgia's Forsyth County. On October 22, 1997, Levi was first playing with his friends. He then rode his bicycle home for dinner, and was abducted on the way, (outside of the county) and was brutally murdered. His case remains unsolved.

Eleven-year-old Levi Frady was last seen on Wednesday, October 22, 1997, on Little Mill Road in Forsyth County. His body was found the next day in the Dawson Forest Wildlife Management Area in Dawson County. Little Mill Road is a well-traveled road between Highway 306 and 369. The Dawson County Sheriff's Office, the Forsyth County Sheriff's Office and the GBI Regional Office in Cleveland are investigating the murder.

Body Found: Dawson Forest Wildlife Management Area in Dawson County Sex: Male

Keeping our Children Safe from sexual predators

Investigators are also seeking the public's help in identifying 2 possible witnesses in the Levi Frady murder case. Anyone with information on the murder of Levi Frady or on the identity of the persons in the sketches is asked to contact the GBI Tip Line at 1-800-597-8477 or by writing: Levi Frady Case189 Highway 53 West, Suite 201
Dawsonville, Georgia 30534

Arkansas: Amber Alert: Morgan Nick

Morgan Nick

The Arkansas alert system is named in honor of Morgan Nick, a six-year-old girl, who was abducted on June 9th, 1995 while she played at an Alma, Arkansas baseball field. Although Morgan has not been located, from the search for this child grew a spirit of dedication from state and community leaders, law enforcement agencies across the state and Colleen Nick, Morgan's mother, to insure Arkansas parents and law enforcement have a means to quickly spread the word when a child is abducted. Relying on the cooperation of the Arkansas radio and television broadcasting industry, the Arkansas State Police has the technical means to interrupt local programming and alert the

Keeping our Children Safe from sexual predators

public of a child's disappearance. A copy of the state's Amber Alert policy can be obtained below in Adobe PDF format.

On the evening of June 9, 1995, Morgan Chauntel Nick was kidnapped while playing with friends just yards away from her mother during a little league game in Alma, Arkansas. A massive investigation ensued, and continues, but Morgan Nick remains missing.

After Morgan's kidnapping it became apparent there was a need for an organization which could provide immediate assistance to the families of missing children.

Colleen Nick, Morgan's mother, realized this need and determined to fight for Morgan and for the hundreds of children that go missing each year; and in 1996, The Morgan Nick Foundation was launched.

The Morgan Nick Foundation (MNF) provides a support network to parents and families of all missing children. The focus of the MNF falls into three categories:

1. Intervention — provided for any family of a missing child. MNF provides on-site support through trained search and rescue workers; prints and disseminates flyers of missing children; works as a liaison with law enforcement and media; coordinates local and national resources for the searching family; provides hope, encouragement, resources,

Keeping our Children Safe from sexual predators

empowerment and on-going support to both the immediate and extended family members of a missing child. MNF also hosts an annual conference entitled Project Hope for families with long-term missing children. The conference focuses on issues surrounding the on-going search.

2. Education — provides FREE safety skills and abduction prevention education to children, parents, teachers and communities. MNF utilizes a safety curriculum entitled "NetSmartz" provided by the National Center for Missing and Exploited Children, as well as the FREE curriculum "Keys to Safety" provided by the Arkansas Attorney General's Office.

3. Legislation — advocating for legislation that protects the rights of children. MNF was instrumental in Federal Mandate signed by President Clinton for Missing Children, as well as the Megan's Law legislation that requires sex offender registration and notification of said registered offender.
The Adam Walsh Child Protection And Safety Act Of 2006
Project Jason-Voice for the Missing: 12/13/05 Campaign for the Missing 2006

The Morgan Nick Foundation believes that to reduce the number of child abductions in the future, we must educate our children and empower them with the skills necessary to protect them from the possible dangers of abduction. We can make a difference… one child at a time. The rights of children and families; a safe environment for children

Jacob Wetterling - Unsolved:

Jacob Wetterling

How We Began and the Need for Transition...

On October 22, 1989, 11-year old Jacob Wetterling was abducted from a group of three boys by a masked gunman. To date, he has never been found and his case remains open. In the flash of precious moments, an unthinkable act occurred that has left an indelible scar on the hearts and minds of Jacob's family, friends and the community.

Many of those same people, including Jacob's parents, decided to turn their anger, sadness and fear into a groundswell of action to protect other children. In 1990, Jacob Wetterling Foundation was formed by Jerry & Patty Wetterling along with many committed members in the community. Their mission was to educate the public about WHO takes children, HOW they do it and WHAT each of us can do to stop it. They turned their pain into action to help innocent children.

Today, people often remark, "I know where I was when Jacob was taken. I remember what I was doing or wearing. I remember how it made me feel. I've never stopped wondering what happened to that little boy." "That defining moment in time continues to impact people throughout Minnesota, Jacob's home state, and in nearly every corner of the world.

Since 1989, many things have changed within our families, community and the world at large. First, came the fax machine, then the Internet, cell phones, two-parent working families and eventually camera phones and iPods. It's no longer a "Father Knows Best or Donna Reed Show" society where there's always a happy ending. Over time, our society has become highly sexualized in what we watch on television, play in video games, see in the media or witness during all types of daily entertainment or interactions.

The public began to ask for laws that would help supervise and rehabilitate convicted sex offenders, so JWF responded by advocating to pass Jacob's Law in Minnesota and throughout the United States. The public needed a missing child emergency response system, so JWF responded, helping to launch the A.M.B.E.R. Plan in Minnesota and at a national level, used in the most severe cases of missing children.

Keeping our Children Safe from sexual predators

Yet some of the difficult changes in the world also brought "new possibilities" that could help reduce the number of children and teens who are abducted or go missing. With the onset of the Internet, mass communications became almost instantaneous when a child went missing....the Internet also brought greater access to child pornography which made it a double-edged sword.

Sometimes children or teens go missing at the hands of non-family members, sometimes at the hand of family members and sometimes they run away from abusive homes to land on the streets where they become prey for those who seek to exploit them. Sometimes they are "thrown away" by those who no longer care about them. Even worse, kids are sometimes "trafficked" for profit or personal gain into things like prostitution, pornography or for the sadistic pleasure of gangs or others who wish to exploit their innocence.

The dramatic changes in our families, communities and the world require new "Tips, Tools & Resources" to combat these unthinkable acts on innocent children. So to honor Jacob's legacy and to respond to the public's outcry, Jacob Wetterling Foundation became Jacob Wetterling Resource Center in September 2008 and launched a new web site to arm the public with the tools they need to help build safer communities for our children and teens.

Keeping our Children Safe from sexual predators

The Jacob Wetterling Resource Center merged with the National Child Protection Training Center in February 2010. The move is an effort to combine the groups' resources and strengthen their common efforts to ensure every child grows up in a healthy, safe world free from abuse, exploitation and abduction.

www.ncptc.org
www.jwrc.org

Keeping our Children Safe from sexual predators

SOME OTHER MISSING ANGELS

Kyron Horman
September 9, 2002
Portland, Oregon,
United States
Disappeared June 4,
2010 (aged 7)

Sierra LaMar Morgan
Hill, CA.
Disappeared Mar 2012
(15 years old)

**Missing: Patrick
Kennedy Alford – 9**
Brooklyn, New
York; Last Seen
January 2010!

*There are still
many others
that are missing
and not listed
here.*

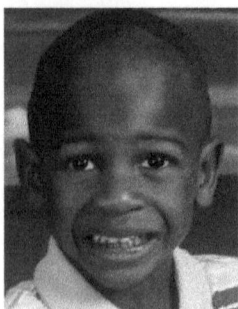

Missing:
Adji Desir-
Immokalee, FL
Age 10,
*Missing Since
2009!*

**Amir Jennings, 1, has
been missing from
Columbia, S.C., since
Nov. 24, 2011**

Keeping our Children Safe from sexual predators

10 Tips a Parent Must Know to Help Keep a Child Safe!

1. Create an open environment with your child so he feels comfortable discussing all matters with you. This will encourage your child to share information he or she may otherwise be embarrassed or shy to tell you.

2. Know where your child is at all times. It's a good idea to have your son or daughter regularly check in with you.

3. Establish a family pass code. In that manner, if you have a message which you wish to convey to your child through a third party, the third party will provide your child with the pass code. Instruct your child never to ask a third party for the family pass code and to keep that password secret. Change your password after using it.

4. Teach your child that it's okay to say "No" to an adult. Children need to know that if something is wrong, it is their right to say no, even to adults, teens and other kids.

5. Make sure your child knows who to call in the event he or she is lost or has an emergency. For example, he or she should know his or her full name, address, home telephone number, your work and cell telephone numbers, additional person he or she can contact such as a grandparent or trusted family friend.

Keeping our Children Safe from sexual predators

6. Tell your child never to keep a secret from you that another adult asks him or her to keep.

7. Instruct your child never to help a stranger who appears to need assistance. Tell your child that the only safe way to help a person in need is to go to a trusted adult or the police. An established and successful trick of many predators is to appear helpless to get the assistance of a child or young adult. For example, serial killer Ted Bundy commonly pretended to have a broken arm in order to abduct young women.

8. Instruct your child never to go with a stranger or acquaintance anywhere alone, visit the house of a stranger or acquaintance alone or allow a stranger or acquaintance into your house when he or she is alone without your prior knowledge and permission. Sometimes children are abused by people whom they casually know. The point is to restrict strangers and acquaintances from having "alone" time with your child.

9. Tell your child to scream "You're not my Mom or Dad" if he or she is approached or threatened by anyone. Children need to know that they should not be embarrassed and need to attract attention to themselves in an emergency.

10. Be willing to discuss safety matters with your child. Create a game for your child so you can present scenarios to test his or her understanding of basic safety rules. The

presentation should be fun and lively so your child is not threatened by the topic, but so he or she continually sharpens his or her skills in taking care of himself or herself.

Note: Although it may appear that your child understands what you have taught him or her, oftentimes children have problems applying the safety rules to factual circumstances. Beware the Unknown includes a section of ready-made scenarios to facilitate this process for teachers, parents and guardians. Studies show that parents can be as effective as trained professionals in teaching their children to protect themselves from offenders. You can make a big difference in keeping your child safe.

These are just a few of the tips that are included and interwoven into the story of Beware the Unknown. Beware the Unknown is a new children's book which teaches kids in a fun way to be safe.

Keeping our Children Safe from sexual predators

A Missing Child Safety Program: What is Code Adam?

Code Adam is a "missing child" safety program in the United States and Canada, originally created by Wal-Mart retail stores in 1994.[1] It is named in memory of Adam Walsh, the 6-year-old son of John Walsh (the host of Fox's America's Most Wanted.). Adam was abducted from a Sears department store in Florida in 1981 and was later found murdered. Today, many department stores, retail shops, shopping malls, supermarkets, amusement parks, hospitals and museums participate in the Code Adam program. Legislation enacted by Congress in 2003 now mandates that all federal office buildings employ the program.

Wal-Mart along with the National Center for Missing & Exploited Children (NCMEC) and the departments of several state Attorneys General, has offered to assist in training workshops in order for other companies to implement the program. Social scientists point out that the fear of child abduction is out of all proportion to its incidence: in particular they point to the long-term persistence of retail kidnapping narratives in urban legends to highlight how parents have been sensitized to this issue for generations before the Adam Walsh case.

Companies that do implement the program generally place a Code Adam decal at the front of the business. Employees at these businesses are trained to do the following six

Keeping our Children Safe from sexual predators

steps according to the National Center for Missing & Exploited Children:

1. If a visitor reports a child is missing, a detailed description of the child and what he or she is wearing is obtained. Additionally, all exterior access to the building is locked and monitored; anyone approaching a door is turned away.
2. The employee goes to the nearest in-house telephone and pages Code Adam, describing the child's physical features and clothing. As designated employees monitor front entrances, other employees begin looking for the child.
3. If the child is not found within 10 minutes, law enforcement is called.
4. If the child is found and appears to have been lost and unharmed, the child is reunited with the searching family member.
5. If the child is found accompanied by someone other than a parent or legal guardian, reasonable efforts to delay their departure will be used without putting the child, staff, or visitors at risk. Law enforcement will be notified and given details about the person accompanying the child.
6. The Code Adam page will be canceled after the child is found or law enforcement arrives.[3]

Keeping our Children Safe from sexual predators

The Adam Walsh Child Protection and Safety Act became law in 2007. This law implements new uniform requirements for sex offender registration across the states (however, these laws can differ in each state). Highlights of the law are a new national sex offender registry, standardized registration requirements for the states, and new and enhanced criminal offenses related to sex offenders. Since its enactment, the Adam Walsh Act (AWA) has come under intense grassroots scrutiny for its far-reaching scope and breadth. Even before any state adopted AWA, several sex offenders were prosecuted under its regulations. This has resulted in one life sentence for failure to register, due to the offender being homeless and unable to register a physical address.[6]

Patty Wetterling, the mother of Jacob Wetterling and a major proponent of the Jacob Wetterling Act, has openly criticized the evolution of sex offender registration and management laws in the United States since the Jacob Wetterling Act was passed, saying that the laws are often applied to too many offenses and that the severity of the laws often makes it difficult to rehabilitate offenders.[9]

Why is "Code Adam" important to your store, your employees, your patrons, and your community? It can be a parent's worst nightmare...suddenly your child is missing. It can happen at an amusement park, a clothing store, a department store, or a supermarket.

Keeping our Children Safe from sexual predators

The Adam Walsh Story:

This is exactly what happened to Revé and John Walsh on July 27, 1981, when their six-year-old son, Adam, was abducted from a Florida department store. Adam and his mother had gone to shop for lamps. The store was about one mile from their home. They parked the car where they usually did. Holding hands, they crossed the parking lot to the entrance, the same as always. That put them in the toy department. Several children were playing with a video, and Adam asked if he could stay and play also. Revé agreed and told him to stay there until she returned from the lamp department. The lamps were about 75 feet - out of sight, but not very far. The lamps were not in stock, so Revé left her name and number. She was gone about seven minutes. Adam was no longer near the video game. Revé walked down several aisles calling out Adam's name. She realized that not only was Adam gone, but all the children were gone and the video game was silent. Revé spotted a boy about Adam's age wearing the same hat as Adam. She asked the child if he had seen another boy with the same hat. He nodded yes, and pointed to the west door. Revé was positive that Adam would not go out the west door. The toy department clerk said she had not seen Adam. Revé started asking anyone she could find, but they all said the same things: Oh well, he probably just wandered off.

I'll bet he went looking for you. Well you know how kids are; maybe he went off with the rest of the kids.

Keeping our Children Safe from sexual predators

*Revé kept insisting that her son did not wander off, and that something was wrong. All around, clerks kept waiting on people as if nothing had happened. She asked a clerk to page her son. "Adam Walsh, please meet your mother in the toy department." Nothing. After going to her car twice to see if Adam had gone there and looking for him on her own for two hours, someone finally called the police department. The police later interviewed a female security guard from the store who said that on the day of Adam's disappearance, there had been four boys playing with the video game in the toy department. They started causing a ruckus. She separated them and sent two boys out the north entrance and two out the west entrance. If Adam had been put out the west entrance he would have been disoriented; he only knew the north entrance. By the end of the first week, 150,000 fliers had been printed and 50,000 of them distributed locally. Adam's photograph was on the poster. The photograph chosen had just been taken the week before and showed a missing tooth. Sixteen days after Adam Walsh disappeared from that local department store; his body was positively identified through dental records and by a friend of the family. To date, no one has been indicted for the abduction and death of Adam Walsh.** This portion is taken from the Book Section, "Tears of Rage," which appeared in Reader's Digest, November 1997 edition - bold face, italicized statements are excerpts from the story with permission from John Walsh*. According to the U.S. Department of Justice, approximately 4,600 children are abducted annually by non-*

Keeping our Children Safe from sexual predators

family members. You can help reduce this number by encouraging your local retailers to adopt the Code Adam program. Your patrons can feel more secure and positive about shopping there. Your employees will have a sense of pride in knowing that they are helping to protect children. Your store will be recognized for its commitment by making the statement, "We Care." We will never know whether or not a "Code Adam" alert in place that July morning in 1981, may have saved Adam's life. Since its development and implementation, Code Adam has successfully stopped eight abductions in progress in Wal-Mart stores across the country. Wal-Mart was the first retail store to implement the program nationwide and the number of stores keeps growing.

John Walsh is the cofounder of the National Center for Missing and Exploited Children and host of Lifetime television's America's Most Wanted: America Fights Back. Code Adam "A Natural Response to Protecting Our Kids"

Stranger Danger

Is "stranger danger"—that dangers to kids come from strangers—really a myth?
Yes. In the majority of cases, the perpetrator is someone the parents or child knows, and that person may be in a position of trust or responsibility to the child and family.

We have learned that children do not have the same understanding of who a stranger is as an adult might, therefore, it is a difficult concept for the child to grasp. It is much more beneficial to children to help them build the confidence and self-esteem they need to stay as safe as possible in any potentially dangerous situation they encounter rather than teaching them to be "on the look out" for a particular type of person.

For decades, parents, guardians, and teachers have told children to "stay away from strangers" in an effort to keep them safe. In response to the on-going debate about the effectiveness of such programs, NCMEC released the research-based Guidelines for Programs to Reduce Child Victimization: A Resource for Communities When Choosing a Program to Teach Personal Safety to Children to assist schools as they select curricula aimed at reducing crimes against children.

For more information on child safety, please visit the More Publications section of this website. Pay particular attention to Child Safety Is More Than a Slogan; Child Protection; and Guidelines for Programs to Reduce Child Victimization: A Resource for Communities When Choosing a Program to Teach Personal Safety to Children.

What other advice can you offer parents about talking to kids?
Parents should choose opportunities or "teachable" moments to reinforce safety skills. If an incident occurs in your community and your child asks you about it, speak frankly but with reassurance.

Keeping our Children Safe from sexual predators

Explain to your children that you want to discuss the safety rules with them, so that they will know what to do if they are ever confronted with a potentially dangerous situation. Make sure you have "safety nets" in place, so that our children know there is always someone who can help them.
What child safety education resources does the National Center for Missing & Exploited Children provide?

The National Center for Missing & Exploited Children offers a wealth of resources to help educate parents, children, law enforcement, and the general public about child safety.

[Safety tips adapted from Know the Rules...General Parental Tips to Help Keep Your Children Safer. Copyright© 2000 National Center for Missing & Exploited Children (NCMEC). All rights reserved.]

Understanding of Consumers:

Consumers need to understand that the first line of defense for families is safety education and line-of-sight supervision of their children. If a device is to be used, understand what it can do and cannot do, that machines can fail, and that the tracking device should be, if they choose, an element within a complete safety program for their family. Ref. NCMEC

Keeping our Children Safe from sexual predators

California Missing Children

California Department of Justice (DOJ) - Reports of Missing Children in California:

1. Runaway refers to a Missing child who has left home without the knowledge or permission of parents or guardian.
2. Lost refers to any child who has strayed away or whose whereabouts are unknown.
3. Catastrophe refers to any child who is missing after a catastrophe (e.g., plane crash, boating accident, fire, flood, etc).
4. Stranger Abduction refers to any witnesses' abduction of a child by a stranger/non-family member.
5. Parental/Family Abduction refers to any child taken by a parent/family member.
6. Suspicious Circumstances refer to any child missing under suspicious circumstances that may indicate a stranger abduction.
7. Unknown Circumstances refer to any child who disappears under circumstances unknown.

Keeping our Children Safe from sexual predators

Ref. California Department of Justice
Missing Children Report of California   2009

Runaways:	100,043
Lost:	268
Catastrophe	22
Stranger Abduction	45
Parental Family Abduction	1,210
Suspicious Circumstances:	349
Unknown Circumstances	3,244
Total:	105,171
Gender: Female:	57,764
Male:	47,407

Keeping our Children Safe from sexual predators

Status of Missing Children Reports in California

1. Returned: Missing child returned on his/her own.
2. Located: Missing child located by law enforcement
3. Deceased: Missing child found deceased
4. Arrested: Missing child arrested
5. Emancipated: Missing juvenile emancipated by the courts.
6. Voluntary Missing: Missing child is voluntary missing
7. Withdrawn/Invalid: Report filed in error or reporting party withdraws report.
8. Other: Report cancelled for reasons other than listed.
9. Unknown: Circumstances why case is cancelled are unknown.

Status of Missing Children Reports in California 2009	
Returned:	69,215
Located:	20,097
Deceased:	61
Arrested	2,786
Emancipated:	107
Voluntary Missing:	89
Withdrawn/Invalid:	629
Other:	5,560
Unknown	72
Total:	98,616

Keeping our Children Safe from sexual predators

Ref. California Department of Justice   2009
Reports of Missing Children by County

Los Angeles
Runaways: 21702
Lost: 50
Castastrophe   2
Stranger Abduction   6
Parental family abduction: 345
Suspicious circumstances   55
Unknown circumstances   904

Total: 23,064

Status of Missing Children Reports by County
_____2009

Los Angeles

Returned: 16167
Located: 2821
Deceased: 5
Arrested: 634
Emancipated   32
Voluntary Missing   13
Withdrawal invalid   73
Other   1,720
Unknown   11

Total: 21,476

Keeping our Children Safe from sexual predators

Reports of Missing Children by County, 2008
Los Angeles

Runaways	23,006
Lost:	37
Catastrophe	6
Stranger Abduction	6
Parental/Family Abduction:	384
Suspicious Circumstances:	38
Unknown Circumstances	1,080
Total:	24,557

Status of Missing Children by County, 2008
Los Angeles

Returned:	16750
Located:	3074
Deceased:	5
Arrested:	675
Emancipated:	15
Voluntary Missing:	22
Withdrawal Invalid:	67
Other	1733
Unknown:	35
Total:	22,376

California Missing Children: Records Found:
385 California: NCMEC
http://www.missingkids.com/missingkids

Keeping our Children Safe from sexual predators

Missing Children Clearinghouse
http://ag.ca.gov/cms_attachments/mups_bulleti
ns/pdfs/m33_4th_qb_20100104.pdf
Have you seen these California Children?
http://dojapp.doj.ca.gov/missing/feature.asp?ac
tion=child

Keeping our Children Safe from sexual predators

Ref: LA County District Attorney's office:
www.da,co.ca.us

Question: What is abduction?
Someone who takes, entices away, keeps, withholds, or conceals a child from lawful custodian or a person with a right to visitation and who did so with the mental state required under the criminal law has broken that law. The law may still be broken in situations where a mother and father have a child together but no custody order exists regarding that child. (California Penal Code sections 278 and 278.5).

Chapter II   Sexual Crimes against Children

Violent Sexual Crimes against Children: A National Crisis:

What is Child sexual Molestation?

- Child sexual molestation and sexual abuse consists of inappropriate and illegal touching of a child in a sexual manner or the sexual exploitation of children by taking pictures and videos of children posed or acting in a sexual manner.

- Child molestation ranges from having the child undress, to touching the child's genitals in a sexual manner, to forcing the child to perform oral sex, to actual sexual intercourse with the child.

- Chronic child molesters prefer either their own gender or the opposite gender as sexual partners. Many times, they understand that their behavior is both unlawful and morally wrong in our society, but they are unable to control their sexual impulses.

- Other child molesters, called pedophiles, don't believe their behavior is wrong and that the child actually enjoys having sex with adults. In summary, child molestation is unlawful sexual contact of any type with a child under the age of consent for sexual acts.

Child Molester

- The term child molester Webster's New World Dictionary defines molest as "annoy, interfere with, or meddle with so as to trouble or harm," it has generally come to convey sexual activity of some type with children.

- Child molester's images brings to mind different individuals: For many it brings to mind the image of the dirty old man in a wrinkled raincoat hanging around a school playground with a bag of candy waiting to lure little children.

- For others, a child molester is one who exposes himself to or fondles children without engaging in vaginal or anal intercourse. For others, a child molester is a stranger to his victim and not a father having sex with his daughter.

- Still others believe the child molester is a nonviolent offender who coax or pressure the child into sexual activity and violent child rapists who overpower or threaten to harm their victims.

- Usually, child molester is a significantly older individual who engages in any type of sexual activity with individuals legally defined as children.

- In some instances, a reported case of a 12 year old child molester requires an investigation of more than just the reported crime. Many people have the concept that the cycle of abuse only means that child victims grow up and become adult offenders.

- It can also mean that the individual can become both a victim and offender at the same time.

Case in Point: A man sexually molests a 13 year old boy. The 13-year old boy goes home and molests his 7 year old brother. The 7 year old brother then molests the baby his mother is babysitting. The investigation of the last activity should lead back to the first crime. (Child molesters: A Behavioral Analysts, pg. 15)

Pedophile

Significantly older Individual who prefers to have sex with individuals legally considered children. Pedophiles are individuals whose erotic imagery and sexual fantasies focus on children. They do not settle for child victims, but in fact, clearly prefer to have sex with children. The law, not puberty, will determine who is a child.

Keeping our Children Safe from sexual predators

Point to remember: While pedophiles prefer to have sex with children, they can and do have sex with adults. Adult sexual relationships are more difficult for some pedophiles than for others. Some pedophiles have sex children. For example one might have occasional sex with a single mother to ensure continued access to her children.

Child Molester versus Pedophile
Not all pedophiles are child molesters. A child molester is an individual who sexually molests children.

A pedophile might have a sexual preference for children and fantasize about having sex with them, but if he does not act on that preference or those fantasies, he is not a child molester.

Some pedophiles might act out their fantasies in legal ways by simply talking to or watching children and later masturbating. Some might have sex with dolls and mannequins that resemble children.

Not all child molesters are pedophiles. A pedophile is an individual who prefers to have sex with children. A person who prefers to have sex with an adult partner may, for any number of reasons, decide to have sex with a child.

Reasons:
1. Simple availability
2. opportunity
3. curiosity

4. Desire to hurt a loved one of the
molested child.

Preferential Patterns of sexual behavior

Situational Type Child Molesters:

Situational type child molester does not usually
have compulsive sexual preferences including
a preference for children. He may, however,
engage in sex with children for varied and
sometimes complex reasons. The situational
type molester usually has fewer child victims.
Other vulnerable individuals such as the elderly
sick or disabled may also be at a risk of sexual
victimization by him. For example, a daycare
center worker who sexually abuses children
might leave that job and begin to sexually
abuse elderly people in a nursing home.

**Three (3) Major Patterns of behavior
emerges here:**
1. Regressed: This person has low self
esteem and poor coping skills; he turns
to children as a sexual substitute for the
preferred peer sex partner. The
availability factor comes into play here
which is why many of these offenders
molest their own children. His MO
(method of Operation) is to coerce the
child into having sex. He may or may
not collect child pornography.

2. Inadequate: This pattern of behavior is
difficult to define and includes those
suffering from psychoses, eccentric

personally disorders, mental retardation, and senility. Simply put, he is the social misfit, the withdrawn, the eccentric loner who still lives with his parents.

Although most individuals are harmless, some can be child molesters and in a few cases, even child killers. This offender seems to become sexually involved with children out of insecurity or curiosity. He finds children to be nonthreatening objects with whom he can explore his sexual interests.

The Child could be someone he knows or a random stranger. In some cases, the child victim might be a stranger selected as a substitute for a specific adult, possibly a relative of the child, whom the offender is afraid of approaching directly.

Because of mental or emotional problems, some might take out their frustration in cruel sexual torture. His victims, however, could be among the elderly as well as children-anyone who appears helpless at first sight. He might collect pornography, but it will most likely be of adults.

3. Morally Indiscriminate:

For this offender the sexual victimization of children is simply part of a general pattern of abuse in his life. He is a user and abuser of people. He abuses his wife, friends, and coworkers. He lies, cheats, or steals whenever he thinks he can get away with it. He molests children for a simple reason- Why not? His primary victim criteria are vulnerability and opportunity. He has the urge, a child an available, and so he acts. He typically uses force; lures, or manipulation to obtain his victims.

He might abduct his victims using trickery or physical force. Although his victims frequently are strangers or acquaintances, his victims can also be his own children or those of his live in girlfriend.

An incestuous father (or mother) might be this morally indiscriminate offender. Because he is an impulsive person who lacks conscience, he is an especially high risk to molest pubescent children. Such acts maybe criminal, but not pornography of a violent nature. He may collect some child pornography especially that which depicts pubescent children. Even when his child victims are acquaintances, he may still use threats and force to overpower of control those victims.

Keeping our Children Safe from sexual predators

Preferential Type Child Molesters

Preferential type child molesters have definite sexual inclinations. For many, their preference includes children, and they are the ones it would be most appropriate to refer to as pedophiles.

Some preferential type sex offenders without a preference for children do, however, molest children. They might do so in order to carry out their bizarre sexual fantasies and preferences with young, less threatening, less judgmental and highly vulnerable victims.

Some of these offenders sexual activity with children may involve deviant acts they are embarrassed or ashamed to request or do with a more experienced adult partner they actually prefer. Such offenders, even if they do not have a sexual preference for children, would still be preferential sex offenders and therefore engage in similar patterns of behavior.

They have the potential to molest large numbers of child victims. For many of them their problem is not only the nature of the sex drive (attraction to children), but also the quantity (need for frequent and repeated sex with children). Preferential type child molesters seem to prefer more boy than girl victims.

Within this category, there are 4 major patterns of behavior emerge: Seduction, Introverted, sadistic, and diverse patterns:

Keeping our Children Safe from sexual predators

1. **Seduction:** This pattern characterizes the offender who engages children in sexual activity by seducing them-grooming them with attention, affection, and gifts. Just as an adult courts another, he seduces children over a period of time by gradually lowering their sexual inhibitions. His victims arrive at the point where they are willing to trade "sex for attention, affection, and other benefits they receive from the offender.

Offenders with a preference for younger children might also spend time seducing the parents. When victimizing such young children, the sex is often made part of a game or horseplay and usually not completely understood as real sex by the children. Most of these offenders are involved with multiple victims.

He knows how to talk to children; he knows how to listen to them. His adult status and authority are also an important part of the seduction.

The biggest problem for this child molester is not how to obtain child victims but how to get them to leave after they are too old. This child molester is likely to use threats and physical violence only to avoid identification and disclosures or prevent a victim from leaving before he is ready to dump the victim. The majority of acquaintance child molesters fall into this pattern of behavior.

2. **Introverted:** This pattern of behavior characterizes the offender who preferences include children but he lacks the interpersonal skills necessary to

Seduce them. He engages in a minimal amount of verbal communication with his victims and usually molests strangers or especially young children.

He is like the old stereotype of the child molester in that he is more likely to hang around playgrounds and other areas where children congregate watching or engaging them in brief sexual encounters. He may expose himself to children or make obscene telephone calls to children. He may utilize the services of a child prostitute, travel to a foreign country, or use the internet to communicate with children.

Unable to figure out any other way to gain access to a child, he might even marry a woman and have his own children, very likely molesting them from the time they are infants. He is similar to the inadequate situational type child molester, except that he has more definite deviant sexual preferences, and acquaintances, but he is far less likely to be involved with multiple victims.

3. **Sadistic:** This pattern of behavior characterizes the offender whose sexual preferences predominately include the need to inflict psychological or physical pain or sufferings on his victims in order to be aroused

or gratified. He is aroused by his victims'
response to the infliction of pain or suffering.
He typically uses lures or force to gain access
to his victims. He is more likely than other
preferential type child molesters to abduct and
even murder his victims. In order to escape
detection, a sexual sadist, even one with
extraordinary interpersonal skills, may try to
abduct victims who are not acquaintances, and
to whom he cannot be linked.

There have been some cases where seduction
acquaintance molesters have become sadistic
molesters. It is not known whether the sadistic
needs developed late or were always here and
surfaced for some reason. Sadistic child
molesters do not appear to be large in number.

4. **Diverse**: This pattern was called the
sexually "indiscriminate" and was under the
situational child molester category. He is the
"try" sexual willing to try anything sexual that
he prefers. The sadistic offender's motivation
in victimizing children is often sexual
experimentation. Such offenders may victimize
children as part of some humiliating taboo, or
forbidden sex. These children maybe his own
or ones he has gained access to through
"marriage." This molester may provide his
children to other adults or use the children of
others as part of group sex spouse-swapping
activity or even as part of some bizarre ritual.
He may be involved in internet communication
with a woman who he encourages to have sex
with her children as part of their "kinky" sex and

let him watch online or send him the visual images.

Child Safety: Community News

A Yearly Catalogue of Some Sexual Crimes Against our Children in Los Angeles and surrounding areas

Note: This list is not complete

1. Anaheim (CBS) — A Santa Ana judge will decide on Thursday whether a convicted child molester should be released on parole.KNX 1070's Mike Landa reports prosecutor Noorul Hasan says Douglas Mackenzie should be committed to a mental hospital because he is a danger to society. Last month he pleaded guilty to molesting and videotaping a 10-year-old boy. He was also investigated for a sex crime in Canada. Mackenzie is eligible for parole because he gets credit for time served in Canadian jail. DA Wants OC Child Molester Committed: February 17, 2011 8:29 AM

2. EL SEGUNDO, Calif. (KABC) -- Officials are warning people in El Segundo about a sexual predator that was seen behind an apartment complex. Police said images of the man were captured on a cell phone camera. He was at an apartment complex on the 300 block of Bungalow Drive on Saturday. Authorities said the suspect was masturbating while watching a toddler playing in a small pool. Anyone with information about the suspect was urged to call El Segundo police at (310) 524-2284. Sexual

Keeping our Children Safe from sexual predators

predator seen at El Segundo apartment: Thursday, August 25, 2011

3. Eight Alleged Gang Members Arrested For Kidnap, Rape of 2 Teen Girls: March 25, 2011 8:49 PM.

4. Fullerton© LA Times: Clown accused of kidnapping and molesting girl faces additional charges: March 28, 2011.

5. Orange County prosecutors Monday filed additional charges against a professional clown arrested Friday on suspicion of kidnapping and raping a girl nine years ago. According to a statement from the district attorney's office, Jose Guadalupe Jimenez, 41, of Anaheim was charged with two felony counts of lewd acts upon a child under 14, one felony count of aggravated sexual assault of a child and one felony count of committing a forcible lewd act on a child under 14. The suspect ran a successful clown business and police said they found numerous costumes and masks at his home. He has been working as a clown for nine years, using the name El Tin Larin.
"We're hoping that any past victims might recognize him, both with or without his clown makeup, and come forward," said Sgt. Andrew Goodrich of the Fullerton Police Department. Police are asking anyone with information to call Det. Kathryn Hamel at (714) 738-5327 or the front desk at (714) 738-6715. Orange County prosecutors Monday filed additional charges against a professional clown arrested

Keeping our Children Safe from sexual predators

Friday on suspicion of kidnapping and raping a girl nine years ago. March, 2011.

6. April 14, 2011: FULLERTON (CBS) — Fullerton police are hoping the public's help will lead them to a man who attempted to sexually assault a 10-year-old girl. Police say the girl was walking along the 2200 block Heterbrink St. when she was approached by a suspect in a black SUV at 12:30 p.m. on April 13.According to police, the suspect persuaded the victim to get in the car where he attempted to sexually assault her. The victim was able to escape and the suspect drove off. The suspect is described as a clean shaven Asian male with black hair. The girl believes her attacker is of Korean decent. He is also described as 17-19 years old, 5 feet 6 inches to 5 feet 8 inches and weighs 150 pounds. The suspect was last seen wearing a white v-neck t-shirt, denim shorts and flip flops. Anyone with information should call Detective L. Markoski at (714) 738-6358 (714) 738-6358 or the Fullerton Police Department's Front Desk at (714) 738-6715 (714) 738-6715

7. Huntington Beach: Michael Joseph DeSilva: 65 years of age. After arresting a registered sex offender who is accused of using his pet parrot as a lure for young children, police are seeking any additional victims of the man.

Authorities are urging anyone who saw the suspect in the Huntington Beach Pier area -- and parents who believe their child came in contact with the man -- to call Huntington Beach police at (714) 960-8825   (714) 960-

Keeping our Children Safe from sexual predators

8825   . Police released a photo of both Michael Joseph DeSilva, 65, of Newport Beach, and his parrot. DeSilva was arrested and booked into the Huntington Beach jail on Saturday. The parrot, named Mango, was taken by Orange County animal control officers, police said. Authorities received a call about 4:15 p.m. of a suspicious man near Main Street and Pacific Coast Highway who was talking to children and trying to get them to play with the parrot.

When police arrived, there were no children present, but upon questioning the man they determined he was a registered sex offender. After contacting his probation officer, police concluded that, based on his activity, DeSilva had violated his probation, Lt. Russell Reinhart said. July, 2011 -- Carla Rivera

8. INDIAN WELLS, Calif. (KABC) -- Officers at the La Quinta Police Department arrested Indian Wells resident Anthony Cornejo Ortiz, 54, on suspicion of committing sex crimes on juvenile males.

The department received a report from a 16-year-old male that he had been sexually assaulted multiple times between May and July in La Quinta and Indian Wells.

Police investigators discovered two other victims, 15 and 17, within the next two weeks.

Police arrested Ortiz Wednesday at about 8:15 a.m. at his Indian Wells residence and served a search warrant there in search of evidence.

Keeping our Children Safe from sexual predators

Ortiz was booked at the Indio Jail for 13 counts of oral copulation; two counts of lewd act with a child, seven counts of sodomy and two counts of furnishing methamphetamine to a minor.

Any person that may be a victim, know of a victim, or anyone with further information about this crime is being asked to contact Investigator Denise Porras at the Sheriff's Indio Station at (760) 863-8990 or email at IndioStation@riversidesheriff.org. Witnesses can also contact Coachella Valley Crime Stoppers at (760) 341-STOP. Informants can remain anonymous and may be eligible for a cash reward.

9. Daycare operator sentenced for sex with teen godson: Wednesday, August 24, 2011.

10. Indian Wells man arrested for teen sexual assaults: Thursday, August 18, 2011.

11. LAKE ELSINORE, Calif. (KABC) -- The search is on for a man who police say sexually battered a high school student as she was heading to school.
The incident happened in Lake Elsinore near Summer hill Drive and Railroad Canyon Road on Friday at about 5 a.m.
The suspect is described as a 20-to 21-year-old black man, between 5 feet 5 inches and 5 feet 6 inches tall, weighing about 160 pounds.

Officials said the suspect sexually battered the girl while she walked to a bus stop and waited for the bus to arrive.

Keeping our Children Safe from sexual predators

Authorities said the suspect was wearing a red hat with white letters, a black shirt, blue jeans and carrying a red backpack.
If you have any information regarding this investigation, you're urged to call the Lake Ellsinore Police Department at (951) 245-3300.

12. LONG BEACH, Calif. (KABC) -- A Santa Monica man is headed to prison for his role in an Internet-based child-pornography ring, a group exploiting kids by stealing their photos and trading them. A law enforcement task force caught up with the porn traders. A specialized task force of Homeland Security investigations joined with LAPD under the umbrella of Immigration and Customs Enforcement to infiltrate the world of the child-pornography trade. Red flags go up with these file names. Some contain images of sexual assaults on children as young as 2 years old. The pictures are prized possessions for Internet porn traders. Monday in federal court, 44-year-old Kevin Wright of Santa Monica was sentenced to seven years in prison. The judge took steps to conceal images of him. Child-porn defendants are often attacked in prison. Wright pleaded guilty to being part of a select group of child-porn traders on an Internet billboard site called Quest4More. "They're collectors. And like a collector of anything, collectibles, it's no fun to collect if you can't share it with someone else," said Claude Arnold, ICE Homeland Security Investigations. When one member got busted, an agent assumed his online identity, leading investigators to four other users. "Polls were taken of the members: 'Would you kidnap

Keeping our Children Safe from sexual predators

a child?'; 'Would you sexually exploit a child who's in your bed?',", said Robert Abrams, ICE Child Exploitation Investigations Group. "Very, very graphic activity was described and elaborated upon." The task force executed search warrants in Los Angeles County arresting scores of people, including a principal, a teacher, a doctor, a lawyer, a scoutmaster, all leading to convictions. "So what you're dealing with these types of offenders is a true psychopathology," said Abrams. "There really is a psychological misfiring going on with these folks." And for the victims it is a never-ending exploitation. The images of their assault are forever circulating online. Forensic investigators are determined to track the pictures. "We are going to find everybody who's touched those, either downloaded images from those sources or posted images up to those sources, and we are going to come after you," said Arnold.

13. Los Angeles: East LA: 01/2011: Man sexually assaulted a 7-year-old boy inside a restroom at a neighborhood Belvedere Park. Details: (A) ABC 7 News: Los Angeles: January 14, 2011, Boy sexually assaulted in Belvedere Park: Facts are as following:

BELVEDERE PARK, EAST LOS ANGELES (KABC) -- A park molester is on the loose. L.A. County Sheriff's deputies are trying to hunt down a man who sexually assaulted a 7-year-old boy inside a restroom at a neighborhood park Saturday.

According to the L.A. County Sheriff's Department, soccer fields at Belvedere Park were full of players and spectators on Saturday at around 6:30 p.m.

A 7-year-old boy told his parents he was going to the restroom. The restroom is just a few feet away from the fields. As he walked into the men's restroom, he was attacked.

"He went into the restroom, and when he did, the suspect immediately entered after him, grabbed him, pushed him into a stall, and sexually assaulted him," said L.A. County Sheriff's Sgt. Diane Hecht.

Sheriff's detectives released a description of the suspect. "The only information we have about the suspect is that he's a male Hispanic, either in his late teens," said Hecht. "He was wearing a red shirt, a red jacket and black-and-white shoes. So we're asking the public, anybody who was at that park who may know the suspect, either way, to contact the sheriff's department."

Off-camera, some parents said they can't believe what happened to the boy. They always felt safe at the park.

14. BOYLE HEIGHTS, LOS ANGELES (KABC) -- A man was arrested after coaxing a 6-year-old girl into an empty school where he sexually assaulted her, according to police. 03/2011

Keeping our Children Safe from sexual predators

15. LOS ANGELES (CBS) — A 28-year-old youth pastor has been charged with multiple counts of sexual molestation for allegedly having a 14-month affair with a teen girl. Demetrius Darnell Allen, of Granada Hills, is charged with 10 counts of lewd act on a child, one count of possession of child pornography and one count of contacting a minor for sexual offense, according to the District Attorney's office. KNX 1070's John Brooks reports. Allen, who works at First Baptist Church in Venice, allegedly began a sexual relationship with the girl, who was 14 at the time, in March of last year.

"The victim was with the church, but the alleged activity did not occur in Venice; it occurred in the San Fernando Valley," said Sandi Gibbons, a spokesperson for the District Attorney's office. He is currently being held on $1 million bail.

16. LOS ANGELES (KABC) -- A 35-year-old female daycare center operator was sentenced to three years in state prison Tuesday for having sex with her 13-year-old godson.

Chelsea McClelland was arrested in December 2010 near the 10 Freeway and La Brea Avenue when area residents reported suspicious activity.
LAPD sexual assault detail officers found McClelland having sex with her godson, who had just turned 13, in the back of a white van. McClelland pleaded no contest on Aug. 2 to two felony counts of lewd act on a child under

14. The incidents occurred between Dec. 1 and Dec. 17, 2010, according to the Los Angeles County District Attorney's Office. In exchange for her plea, two additional counts of lewd act on a child were dismissed, according to the DA.

In addition to her prison sentence, McClelland was also ordered to register as a sex offender for the rest of her life.

17. LOS ANGELES (KABC) -- A local soccer coach was arrested for allegedly molesting his players, and police say there could be more victims. Authorities said 42-year-old Jose Duarte formed and sponsored his own team called U.S.A., which practiced and played in MacArthur Park, Vista Hermosa Park and Gilbert Lindsey Recreation Center in South Los Angeles. Duarte is charged with 15 counts of felony child molestation. Officials said the molestation had gone on for at least one year. A 13-year-old victim came forward Sunday to say he had been sexually assaulted by his soccer coach. Police said Duarte committed the sexual assault at his house and his car.

The LAPD's Sexual Assault Detail team has since identified two other victims, who say they've also been coached and molested by Duarte. "Wow. I can't believe someone would do that," said 16-year-old Lourdes Tran. Tran and members of a healthy eating group exercising at MacArthur Park were surprised by Duarte's arrest. Tran said one member's son plays soccer in the park and is concerned he may have had contact with Duarte. Adults playing a pick-up game Thursday morning said kids usually practice after school and play their games on Saturday. Players told Eyewitness News that they didn't recognize Duarte's picture but they're glad police made an arrest. In addition to coaching, authorities said Duarte also helped transport kids at Webster Middle School for soccer practice. Bail for Duarte has been set at $2.5 million. There may be more victims out there. If you have any information regarding this case, please call (877) LAPD-24-7 or (877) 527-3247. June 30, 2011

18. LOS ANGELES (KABC) -- A Compton man has been arrested for allegedly inappropriately touching young girls at a local pool. Lifeguards said they saw Darnell Island, 32, touching the girls, who ranged in age from 9 to 13, at the Ted Watkins Memorial Park pool on East 103rd Street in Watts. The lifeguards called sheriff's deputies, who found four victims who said they had been approached and touched by Island. Island is being held on $100,000 bail. July, 2011

19. Manhattan Beach: MANHATTAN BEACH (CBS) — a 76-year-old Manhattan Beach man has been arrested for allegedly molesting three girls.
Ronald Balmayne was arrested at his home July 26, said Stephanie Martin of the Manhattan Beach Police Department.
Police believe there are potentially more victims.
The district attorney's office has filed two counts of lewd acts upon a child and one count

of sexual exploitation of a child against Balmayne, Martin said.

"Manhattan Beach detectives recently investigated Balmayne for sexual molestation of female children from 1981-2002," Martin said in a statement.

"At this time, three victims have been identified."

Police urged anyone who believes their child has had contact with Balmayne to contact Manhattan Beach Police Detective John Loy at (310) 802-5121. August 4, 2011.

20. Moreno Valley BY ALIYAH SHAHID DAILY NEWS STAFF WRITER
Tuesday, March 29, 2011 an 11-year-old girl was lured into a park restroom and raped by seven members of a Southern California gang, according to authorities. Moreno Valley, about 70 miles east of Los Angeles. The six others - all juveniles - allegedly involved Suspect Michael Sykes, 19, was arrested on Monday in Mo in the shocking crime were taken into custody shortly after the March 10 attack. The crime was made public earlier this week. The horror began at a shopping center when an older girl talked the young victim into going in the Victoriano Park's bathroom In Moreno Valley. The older girl, who has since been arrested, led the 11-year-old to the bathroom, where the boys and Sykes were waiting around 6 p.m

21. Moreno Valley: Lovetta Poole has been charged with three counts of lewd acts with a child under the age of 14 and two counts of

Keeping our Children Safe from sexual predators

aggravated sexual assault. This is from the booking information from the Riverside County Sheriff's Department. 04/2011

22. Monteclair MONTCLAIR (CBS) — A choir director of a Southland church was arrested Sunday after being caught with an under aged girl. According to Montclair police, Mark Michaels of Upland was arrested and booked at the West Valley Detention Center on charges of oral copulation and lewd and lavivious acts with a child. Early Sunday morning, Michaels, 53, was found with the teenaged girl inside a vehicle, according to Montclair police. An officer reportedly observed inappropriate sexual activity. When the vehicle tried to drive away, police conducted a traffic stop and found Michaels and the girl in the car, officials said.

After an investigation, authorities determined that Michaels and the girl, 15, knew each other from their church. Investigators say the girl was a member of the church's choir and she had known Michaels for two years. The teen was later remanded to her parents. At the time of Michael's arrest, he was the part-time choir director at Bethany Baptist Church in Montclair. He was fired Sunday night by church elders. Michaels is being held on a $50,000 bail. He will make his first court appearance Tuesday. Investigators are trying to determine if there are additional victims.

23. PALMDALE, Calif. (KABC) -- Neighbors of an 80-year-old registered sex offender who

Keeping our Children Safe from sexual predators

was arrested Saturday for allegedly trying to kidnap a girl say the news came to them as no surprise. Keith Wayne Holmes was taken into custody for allegedly trying to lure a 12-year-old girl into his vehicle by offering her a ride on Pearblossom Highway and 85th Street. When she refused, he allegedly continued to drive slowly alongside her. "At that point the mother of the victim was alerted and asked what was going on," said Dep. John Gilbert of the Los Angeles County Sheriff's Department. "The suspect drove away in rapid fashion. A witness was able to obtain a license plate." When deputies stopped Holmes a short time later, they searched the car and found duct tape, gloves and rope. Holmes said he uses those items for his hobby of building boats at his home. Holmes, who was on probation for a 2009 conviction of annoying or molesting a child, denies talking to the girl. When asked if he was going to harm the girl, Holmes said, "No. God knows, so help me God."

"I've actually seen him driving around in his little truck actually looking to pick up kids," neighbor Charity Mackiwicz said. Holmes lives in the unincorporated Los Angeles town of Pearblossom, just one block from Pearblossom Elementary School. June, 2011

24. By Staff, City News Service
Thursday, March 10, 2011 Perris man charged with sexually assaulting 10-year-old girl A Perris man was charged today with sexually assaulting a 10-year-old girl he may have used to make child pornography

Keeping our Children Safe from sexual predators

William Riley Ward, 30, was expected to be arraigned this afternoon on one count each of forced oral copulation of a child 10 years or younger, lewd acts on a child under 14 and possession of child pornography. While investigators were at the location, they uncovered "evidence revealing ... recent, repeated sexual victimization of a 10-year-old Perris-area child," Smith alleged. "This victimization was previously unreported and unknown to law enforcement."
Also taken into custody during the investigation was Ward's friend, 44-year-old Gregory Lawrence Noble, who was booked on suspicion of lewd and lascivious conduct with a child. He posted a $50,000 bond and was released from the Robert Presley Detention Center in Riverside on Wednesday.

25. PICO RIVERA, Calif. (KTLA) -- Authorities are searching for the man who sexually assaulted a 6-year-old boy in a bathroom at park in Pico Rivera. The boy reported being molested in a bathroom stall just after 2:30 p.m. Saturday at Rio Hondo Park. Sheriff's officials say the boy was at the park with family members for a soccer match when he went into the bathroom alone. The boy's mother apparently realized her son was missing for about 10 minutes and went looking for him. July 4, 2011 (KTLA)

26. A 23-year-old Perris-area man accused of molesting his ex-girlfriend's 3-year-old daughter and taking cell phone photos of the

assault pleaded not guilty this week, court records say. 04/15/11

27. Redlands: Grove High School student charged with sexual assault (53%) 01/21/2011 - REDLANDS - An 18-year-old student at Grove High School has been arrested and charged with sexually assaulting two female students at or near the school in the last three months.

28. REDDING (AP) — A Northern California man who appealed for his missing teenage daughter's return on national television has pleaded not guilty to molesting her. The Redding Searchlight reports that 33-year-old Jacob Berlinghoff of Redding entered not guilty pleas Monday to a felony count of lewd and lascivious behavior with a child under 14 and misdemeanor counts of annoying a child and sexual battery. He is free on $50,000 bail.

The newspaper reports that shortly after the 15-year-old girl returned from a 31-day disappearance with her uncle last year, she accused her father of fondling her. She said the 2008 incident was one of the reasons she fled. Her uncle, 44-year-old Charles Berlinghoff, is facing nearly 100 sex abuse charges involving the teen. He remains jailed on $1.6 million bail.

29. A San Bernardino County sheriff's deputy was arrested and placed on administrative leave late Friday, the same day the department received information he may have had sexual

relations with a 16-year-old girl, according to a Sunday news release. 04/2011

30. Thursday, April 21, 2011 VENTURA, Calif. (KABC) -- Authorities announced that they have made an arrest in a rash of sexual battery cases near a middle school in Ventura. Oxnard resident Luis Sanchez-Vega is accused of approaching women and teenagers on the street and fondling them. The victims ranged in age from 13 to 38.

31. San Clemente: Church Volunteer: Arrested: SAN CLEMENTE (CBS) — a church volunteer was arrested in Texas Friday on suspicion of molesting a San Clemente girl more than 15 years ago.

Joe David Nelms, 47, of Lindale, Texas, allegedly molested the girl between 1993 and 1996, starting when the girl was under 14, Orange County Sheriff's spokesman Jim Armomino said. At the time, the girl lived with her family in San Clemente and attended Pacific Coast church.

The victim, who is now in her 30s, went to authorities March 4 after working up the courage, Armomino said. The woman said she reached out to a former youth counselor who advised her to make a police report.

The woman says Nelms molested her in a church office, while driving around San

Clemente and in his home in San Clemente, Armomino said.

At the time of his arrest, Nelms worked as a volunteer teacher for high school students at the First Baptist Church of Lindale. He also worked with high school students at Sky Ranch, a company that hosts retreats, Armomino said. Nelms was forced to resign from his pastor job when the senior pastor became aware of the allegations.

32. SANTA ANA (CBS) — A 32-year-old Santa Ana man pleaded guilty Friday to having sex and smoking pot with a 12-year-old girl.

Neftali Pena Procopio pleaded guilty to two felony counts of lewd acts on a child under 14 and a felony count of giving marijuana to a child, and admitted sentencing enhancement allegations for substantial sexual conduct with a child.

Procopio was arrested about 2 a.m., Aug. 17, in the 200 block of South Ross Street after he was found having sex with the girl in the back seat of his car, Santa Ana police Cpl. Anthony Bertagna said.

The two reportedly met Aug. 16 at Santa Ana High School, where they were playing in separate basketball games, Bertagna said.

The two made plans to meet later that night. The minor snuck out of the house and the two had a long conversation before having sex,

Keeping our Children Safe from sexual predators

Bertagna said. An officer driving by about 2 a.m. saw fogged up windows in the car and used condoms outside the vehicle. He then looked into the vehicle and saw the two naked in the back seat, Bertagna said. Sentencing was scheduled for April 1. Procopio faces up to 11 years and eight months in prison.

33. Missing Girl's Father, Uncle Accused of Sexually Molesting Her: January 31, 2011 5:21 PM.

34. Santa Ana Man, 32, Guilty Of Having Sex, Smoking Pot With Girl, 12:

35. Santa Ana man arrested for sex trafficking: Monday, August 15, 2011

SANTA ANA, Calif. (KABC) -- An Orange County man was charged with sex trafficking after the rescue of three teenage girls.

Investigators say Santa Ana resident Samuel Martinez Gonzalez picked up the girls in Texas with the promise he would take them to the beach.

He allegedly forced them to work as prostitutes in Southern California.

One of the girls was allegedly found with Gonzalez, and the other two were found at a local hotel. The girls are now in protective custody.

Keeping our Children Safe from sexual predators

36. Simi Valley man arrested for sex with 12-year-old girl: Friday, August 19, 2011 SIMI VALLEY, Calif. (KABC) -- Simi Valley police officers arrested Thursday a 22-year-old man on suspicion of unlawful sex with a 12-year-old.

Simi Valley resident Spencer Neminski, 22, was arrested Thursday afternoon while walking the 5000 block of Arroyo Lane. Neminski was charged with lewd/lascivious acts with a minor and was booked at the Ventura County Jail.

The 12-year-old female victim went to the Simi Valley Police Department with her mother Wednesday to report the crime.

The victim told police that on Aug. 11, she met Neminski through friends, and that they agreed to meet that night at his vehicle parked on the 5000 block of Arroyo Lane.

The two engaged in consensual sexual acts in the vehicle, according to police. The girl eventually told an adult neighbor about the encounter, which then told the girl's mother.

37. Girl sexually attacked on way to school in Lake Elsinore
38. Sunday, August 28, 2011 Santa Ana: SANTA ANA (CBS) — A children's book writer from San Clemente was behind bars Thursday on suspicion of having sex with an underage girl for nearly a year, an Orange County sheriff's spokesman said. Michael Snyder, 43, was arrested about 7 p.m. Wednesday as he

was picking up his children at the Boys and Girls Club in San Clemente.

The girl told her mother about the alleged relationship with Snyder, and her mother alerted authorities on Wednesday, officials said. He is the author of children's books and has been involved with after- school programs so we're concerned ... We don't know what kind of access he has to children," Orange County sheriff's spokesman Jim Amormino said.

Snyder also owns a company that subcontracts with the state Department of Developmental Services to provide services for mentally and physically disabled people and their families, Amormino said. On Snyder's children's book website — beetlebugbooks.com — he is identified as Mr. Mike, and the list of books includes, "Lemon Drop Rain," "Swimming In Chocolate" and "Over the Top."Snyder was being held on $100,000 bail on suspicion of child molestation.

39. SANTA CLARITA, Calif. (KABC) -- A man suspected in a sexual assault against a child in a shopping mall was arrested Tuesday. The suspect surrendered to L.A. County Sheriff's deputies Tuesday less than 24 hours after he allegedly molested an 11-year-old boy in a mall bathroom. Police had identified the man as a suspect in the molestation, which allegedly happened Monday at the Westfield Mall in Valencia. The same suspect was arrested a week ago on another assault case.

Keeping our Children Safe from sexual predators

According to the sheriff's department, an 11-year-old boy was using the public restroom in the food court area Monday at about 4 p.m. when a stranger sexually assaulted him. The boy's father then confronted the suspect. Investigators later identified the suspect as 25-year-old Casey Crockett. According to investigators, the boy's father got into a physical fight with Crockett after hearing about what happened in the restroom, but Crockett took off running in the direction of a transit center across the street. The Special Victims Bureau of the sheriff's department began a search for Crockett. We went to the home where he lives with his parents earlier today. No one answered the door at the residence where Crockett lives with his parents. Neighbors were shocked to hear what he was accused of. Crockett surrendered to sheriff's deputies less than 24 hours later.

A mall representative said they are cooperating with the investigation, and the safety and security of shoppers remains the mall's priority.

40. SANTA PAULA (CBS/AP) — Several alleged gang members were arraigned Tuesday afternoon on sex crimes charges after police say they used social media websites to kidnap and rape young girls.

The seven adults and one juvenile were arrested Friday. The suspects were identified as Carlos Ek, 22; Esteban Oseguera, 18; Isaac Ek, 19; Joseph Sandoval, 18; Jonathan Gaona, 19; Dion Mendoza, 19;

Keeping our Children Safe from sexual predators

Adrian Garcia, 19, and a 17-year-old juvenile, all of Santa Paula.

Six of the eight suspects were arraigned Tuesday in Ventura County court on charges ranging from rape, conspiracy, child abuse, sexual battery by restraint and parole violations. An additional suspect arrested in connection with the assaults was not immediately charged.

Carlos Ek was arrested on suspicion of attempted murder for a Solimar Beach stabbing being investigated by the Ventura County Sheriff's Department. It was unclear if he was arraigned Tuesday on those charges.

Authorities say they were familiar with the suspects due to their alleged gang ties.

The arrests were the result of a six-week investigation of two rapes that occurred in March and April.

Santa Paula police said the suspects used the Internet to lure teenaged girls to house parties where they were given alcohol, possibly drugged and then raped by multiple men. Authorities say at least one rape occurred while the victim was sleeping.

"Its pretty clear right now that alcohol was involved. The bottom line is they can really become incapacitated and abused anyway and they just didn't know this was going to happen," said Santa Paula Police Chief Stephan MacKinnon.

Authorities have investigated two known cases, but fear there could be more victims who haven't come forward. Ventura County prosecutors say they will seek to try the 17-year-old as an adult. June 7, 2011 5:49 AM

41 THOUSAND OAKS, Calif. (KABC) -- A Newbury Park man was arrested Thursday on suspicion of possessing child pornography. The Thousand Oaks Police Department and FBI arrested Verl Darvin Chaney, 52. The investigation began in May when an undercover Thousand Oaks police detective using a publicly available file-sharing program found that Chaney was sharing illegal child pornography. The downloaded images and videos contained actual minors engaging in sexually explicit conduct, police said. A search warrant was served at Chaney's home and he was arrested without incident. He was booked on felony child pornography into the Ventura County Jail with bail set at $50,000. July 3, 2011

42. History Teacher: Arrested: VAN NUYS (CBS) — A 29-year-old history teacher at Montclair College Preparatory School in Van Nuys was arrested Monday for allegedly engaging in a sexual relationship with a 15-year-old girl.

Gazi Kabir was taken into custody by detectives from the Los Angeles Police Department's Van Nuys Division.

Keeping our Children Safe from sexual predators

Police alleged that Kabir would periodically go to the girl's house when she was alone, and suspect there may be other alleged victims. Anyone with information relevant to the case was asked to call detectives at (818) 374-0040.

43. Thursday, April 21, 2011 VENTURA, Calif. (KABC) -- Authorities announced that they have made an arrest in a rash of sexual battery cases near a middle school in Ventura. Oxnard resident Luis Sanchez-Vega is accused of approaching women and teenagers on the street and fondling them. The victims ranged in age from 13 to 38.

44. Union: Eugene Melendres Ramos, Charged With Rape of 2-Year-Old,

By Joe Eskenazi, Mon., Dec. 6 2010 @ 7:45AM

Eugene Melendres Ramos, the Union City man who shocked the nation when he was allegedly caught in the act of raping a 2-year-old in an East Bay Dollar Tree, will be in front of a judge today.

Ramos did not enter a plea on Friday and is due back at the Fremont Hall of Justice this morning. The 36-year-old is charged with committing a forcible lewd act with a child younger than 14; assault with intent to commit a sex crime; and attempted intercourse or sodomy with a child younger than 10. His 2005 conviction for sexually assaulting a child could count as a prior "strike." He could face up to 21 years if convicted.

45. LAUSD, Los Angeles Unified School District: Set of Teacher-Student Sexual Abuse allegations: **LAUSD & other School districts: Allegations of Sex Abuse**

- *Teacher accused of Allegations against a veteran Miramonte Elementary instructor leave many parents shocked and angry. The probe that led to 23 counts involving kids 7 to 10 began after disturbing photos were reported.*
- 2nd Teacher: accused of sexual abuse allegations: Miramonte Elementary
- Los Angeles Female Teacher Aide: Love letter allegedly from teacher's aide: Miramonte Elementary
- Hamilton High School: Allegations teacher had sex with students
- Telfair Elementary School in Pacoima: Allegations of 3rd grade teacher of sex abuse to 4 students
- A Janitor at Germain Elementary School in Chatsworth, was arrested Monday on suspicion of committing a lewd act.
- A teacher's aide from John C. Fremont High School in South L.A. has been arrested by the FBI.
- *LAUSD Substitute teacher quit after the third inquiry and started working in Inglewood schools. Police later found video of him molesting a girl in that district; he was charged, but he fled and is at large.*
- COMPTON: Compton middle school. teacher is under investigation in an alleged sexual misconduct case. The

latest allegations involve an unidentified male teacher and a female student at Davis Middle School. For now, the teacher has been removed from the school.

- **MONTEBELLO (CBS)** — Police Thursday announced the arrest of a female Roosevelt High School Spanish teacher on suspicion of having sex with two students — the latest of several sexual scandals to bedevil the Los Angeles Unified School District.

- Hawthorne: A high school band teacher remains jailed on suspicion of having unlawful sex with a 17-year-old girl. Teacher was arrested Monday after the alleged victim and her mother reported to the Hawthorne Police Department that the student had sex with the suspect at his home, according to Hawthorne Police Department Lt. Scott Swain

- RUNNING SPRINGS, Calif. (KTLA) -- FBI agents arrested a San Bernardino middle school teacher Tuesday morning, claiming he exchanged sexually-explicit images with a 13-year-old New Jersey girl

- **HEMET (CBS)** — Deputies arrested a female Hemet High School teacher Thursday and accused her of having sex with a male student on campus, a sheriff's department spokesman said.

- La Mirada, Los Coyotes Middle School, A Substitute educator, was arrested yesterday after a 6th grade student said the teacher touched her inappropriately.

- NORTH HILLS) -- The Los Angeles Unified School District has removed another teacher following allegations of inappropriate behavior. The teacher worked at Lassen Elementary School in North Hills.
- CHINO, Calif. (KABC) -- A 5th grade teacher from Walnut Elementary School in Chino has been arrested for alleged lewd acts on a child.
- SANTA ANA, Calif. (KABC) -- An ex-choir teacher at an Orange County catholic school has been convicted of child molestation. Prosecutors say in 2008, Hong Luong molested a female student when he worked at Saint Callistus Catholic School in Garden Grove.

46. Boy Scouts of America: Sex Abuse allegations

AP) — Again and again, decade after decade, an array of authorities — police chiefs, prosecutors, pastors and local Boy Scout leaders among them — quietly shielded scoutmasters and others accused of molesting children, a newly opened trove of confidential papers shows.

At the time, those authorities justified their actions as necessary to protect the good name and good works of Scouting, a pillar of 20th century America. But as detailed in 14,500 pages of secret "perversion files" released Thursday by order of the Oregon Supreme Court, their maneuvers allowed sexual predators to go free while victims suffered in silence.

The files are a window on a much larger collection of documents the Boy Scouts of America began collecting soon after their founding in 1910. The files, kept at Boy Scout headquarters in Texas, consist of memos from local and national Scout executives, handwritten letters from victims and their parents and newspaper clippings about legal cases. The files contain details about proven molesters, but also unsubstantiated allegations.

47. Catholic Church Sexual Abuse: Los Angeles

Evidence shows bold L.A. priest abuse cover-up

Jan 22, 2013: (CBS News) LOS ANGELES - There is new evidence that leaders of the Catholic Church in Los Angeles maneuvered secretly to shield priests accused of sexually abusing children.

Documents just released indicate they never told parishioners -- or the police -- what they knew.

Keeping our Children Safe from sexual predators

"What we're seeing in these files is but a glimpse into a very, very dark, and endless tunnel of secrecy, of abuse, of silence," said Raymond Boucher, a former altar boy and current lead attorney, representing some 500 victims of sex abuse by priests in the archdiocese of Los Angeles.

Files show L.A. archdiocese manipulation in abuse cases
Judge to church: Keep names in Los Angeles priest abuse files
Ten years after revelations of massive sex abuse cover-ups, many victims never get their day in court

48. Catholic Church Sexual Abuse: Philadelphia

June 22, 2012: PHILADELPHIA -- A Roman Catholic church official was convicted Friday of child endangerment but acquitted of conspiracy in a groundbreaking clergy-abuse trial, becoming the first U.S. church official convicted of a crime for how he handled abuse claims.

Monsignor William Lynn helped the archdiocese keep predators in ministry, and the public in the dark, by telling parishes their priest was being removed for health reasons and then sending the men to unsuspecting churches, prosecutors said.

Lynn, 61, had faced about 10 to 20 years in prison if convicted of all three counts he faced

– conspiracy and two counts of child endangerment. He was convicted only on one of the endangerment counts, leaving him with the possibility of 3 1/2 to seven years in prison.

He has been on leave from the church since his arrest last year. He served as secretary for clergy from 1992 to 2004, mostly under Cardinal Anthony Bevilacqua.www.washingtonpost.com

49. Church Sex Abuse: Oct. 18, 2012: WASHINGTON -- Three female plaintiffs claim an evangelical church group covered up allegations of sexual abuse against children, failed to report accusations to the police and discouraged its members from cooperating with law enforcement, according to a lawsuit filed Wednesday.

The lawsuit was filed in Maryland state court against Sovereign Grace Ministries, a 30-year-old family of churches with more than 80 congregations. Most of its churches are in the U.S., but it also has planted congregations in other countries. The alleged abuse happened in Maryland and northern Virginia in the 1980s and 1990s.

The plaintiffs allege a conspiracy spanning more than two decades to conceal sexual abuse committed by church members. They accuse church representatives of permitting suspected pedophiles to interact with children, supplying them with free legal advice to avoid prosecution and forcing victims to meet with and "forgive" the person that had molested them.

"The facts show that the Church cared more about protecting its financial and institutional standing than about protecting children, its most vulnerable members," the lawsuit claims.

50. Church of God in Christ sexual abuse allegations

(a) North Carolina: December 2012: Good news as justice is finally being served against the former North Carolina COGIC Supt Thomas Wiggins, Jr. who sexually abused a 14 year old boy all while he was "preaching", pastoring two churches and climbing his denomination's ecclesiastical ladder. The Star News Online reported on Monday that Wiggins is headed to prison to serve between 6 and 9 years for his crimes. See our previous coverage on Thomas Wiggins here and here. A Wilmington pastor pleaded guilty to six counts of felony sexual abuse of a minor by a substitute parent during a hearing in New Hanover County Superior Court on Monday.

Thomas Archie Wiggins, 55, a pastor at Wilmington's Faith Temple Church of God in Christ, was sentenced to between six years and three months and nine years and nine months in prison. He was taken into custody Monday.

Keeping our Children Safe from sexual predators

After serving the sentence, the Wilmington resident also must register as a sex offender for 30 years.

Wiggins was arrested in November 2011 and charged with five counts of first-degree sexual offense and five counts of indecent liberties with a minor after he admitted to abusing a then 14-year-old boy who had been in his care during 1998 and 1999, New Hanover County Assistant District Attorney Lance Oehrlein said during the hearing.

http://cogicabusewatch.wordpress.com/2012/12/05/cogic-sex-abuser-thomas-wiggins-headed-to-prison-for-6-9-years/

Updates on COGIC molestation case in Virginia

Year after year, **pedophiles continue to pop** up all over COGIC despite the warning of Presiding Bishop Charles Blake to "get right or get out". And although a new election swept in some new church leaders, the issue of pedophilia, child sex crimes and its resultant issues were all but ignored.

(b) After posting the story of Don Billups, the deacon at Gospel Tabernacle COGIC in Covington, VA who was convicted of molesting at **least 8 children**, some clarifications are in order to properly identify individuals connected to the case. The case has devastated the population of this small town of about 3000 along the West Virginia-Virginia border. Billups was a well known figure in the town. The current pastor of Gospel Tabernacle is Gregory P. Moore. Billups was under Moore's supervision for two years prior to the conviction. After the story broke in the media, Moore took a book called "Mercy for the molester" to one family, telling them that they had to "forgive the molester". During the trial, Moore also testified on behalf of Billups.

(c). Local news media did not report that Moore is also in legal trouble for a separate incident involving a gun threat.

(d). Gospel Tabernacle is currently in the Greater West Virginia Jurisdiction where Henderson Wheeler is bishop. The church was previously pastored by Supt. Warner L. Hunter, until his death in 2009 until Moore, his son-in-law became pastor.

(e). Although Billups was only convicted of 8 molestations, there were more children whose parents did not want them to testify thus were excluded from the case against him. Some of the children had grown up in the church and knew Billups and his family.

(f). Sources informed Report COGIC Abuse that the bishop, Henderson Wheeler since news of the molestation broke had visited once but told the victim's families he was "praying for them". He has not visited nor spoken with victims since the case became public. In a perverted fashion, COGIC leadership treats victims as if they are the criminals. Family members were told by the jurisdictional supervisor that she was forbidden by the bishop to have contact with them. Past cases in Asheville NC, Newark, Winter Haven FL, Albany NY and Kalamazoo MI reveal the same pattern of post crime behavior by COGIC leaders.

(g) New information also reveals that Billups, a retired Marine, was the head deacon at Gospel Tabernacle for many years and his wife a leading "missionary.

(h) Report COGIC Abuse will continue to update this story as information becomes available. A listing of Billups' charges from Alleghany County Circuit Court.

Breaking news: COGIC deacon in VA convicted of molesting 8 children

(i) COGIC's newly re-elected —and clearly frustrated— Presiding Bishop Charles Blake issued a strong rebuke to pedophiles embedded across the denomination's landscape during his 2012 official message in St. Louis [video].

"The church has got to be a safety zone for our children. If you are a pedophile, if you are a child molester, if you are a child abuser, if you are determined to pursue sexual misconduct, then either get right or get out. Get right or get out!"

Keeping our Children Safe from sexual predators

Met with tepid applause, the statement may reveal that the church and its leader still aren't aware of exactly what they are dealing with. Pedophiles have no intention of getting right. Or getting out. And although speeches sound good in a preach to the choir kind of way, they have proven ineffective against determined pedophiles with power and positions juxtaposed against weak, excuse-laden church leaders.

(J) Most church pedophiles rack up numerous victims while using their positions as cover for their nefarious activities. Just like Don Billups, a deacon at Gospel Tabernacle COGIC in Covington, VA. After a jury found him guilty of molesting *at least* eight children, they recommended two life sentences, plus 75 years for his sex crimes. Some of the victims were under age 13, WSLS reported. Some of the cases dated back to 2002. Billups was arrested in May 2012.

(K) Elder Gregory P. Moore [see update/clarifications], the pastor had only been in place 2 years. He told reporters he put Billings out of the church *when the allegations came to light*. But how does a child molester remain in a leadership position for **10 years** of more at a Church of God in Christ with so many victims and no one knows he is constantly molesting children? Bishop Blake's strong words may be too little, too late for thousands of abused children at the hands of COGIC leaders. If outside legal and law enforcement intervention is what it will take to

Keeping our Children Safe from sexual predators

break the unshaken cycle, children in COGIC are in dire trouble. They church's leadership doesn't seem to posses the fortitude handle it internally. Bishop Blake and his administration are notorious for window dressing while they continually ignore the voice of real victims and their families. Billups will be formally sentenced on February 19, 2013. Report COGIC Abuse will update this blog with his sentencing.

(I) 2012: COGIC officials in Albany NY kept pedophile elders secret: St Johns COGIC; Wilborn Temple COGIC. Albany New York: September 2012: Beginning in the late 70s, Church of God in Christ officials in New York's capital city knew about multiple child sex abuses committed by five different pedophiles. Instead of protecting children, church officials shielded the pedophiles and concealed their crimes. In one case, three generations of family members had been sexually molested. Two of the pedophile elders were in position at Wilborn Temple COGIC, the other three at St Johns COGIC. That's what a lengthy and detailed letter made public last month, alleges. The two stately looking, in town churches have for decades harbored pedophiles that preyed on a still undetermined number of children.

Written by Christopher Davis, a project management consultant and son of a local COGIC pastor in Albany, New York, the letter characterized what he had uncovered as a "coming storm" due to the layers of deceit and ignorance of the Albany COGIC community

Keeping our Children Safe from sexual predators

"You can choose to ignore this coming storm and leave yourself to its perils or you can arm yourself with knowledge, understanding and wisdom. You can choose to think for yourself or let someone else think for you, but know in your choice is your fate. Know and understand that in judgment you stand alone and on your works and your deeds. The single thing which separates man from all of God's creations is the ability of cognitive thought; it is this in which we are made in His image. In relinquishing your right and responsibility to think for yourself you have forsaken your humanity and in turn you have forsaken God who created you in His image."

Davis, who now lives in New Jersey, said that he came upon the decades long sexual abuse situations while he was in the process of helping a church deal with rebuilding after fire damage.

"In January 2012 Blessed Hope Worship Center, a COGIC affiliate under Pastor Ronald Howard, experienced a fire which damaged their church home on Central Avenue in Albany, New York. The damage to the church was extensive and Pastor Howard recognized his limitations in navigating the church through the many hurdles they would have to face in rebuilding. Through then Superintendent and Pastor James Davis, Pastor Howard contacted me, to ask for my assistance in their endeavors to rebuild."

Keeping our Children Safe from sexual predators

(L) Conversations with Howard eventually revealed an incidence of pedophilia committed against a 10 year old boy of which the perpetrator was still an active COGIC leader.

Davis told Report COGIC Abuse that despite damning evidence he presented (including the personal testimony of a victim), he encountered a shocking corporate attitude among COGIC leaders, including Western New York First jurisdiction Bishop James R. Wright. Most of the leaders showed more concern for the doctrine and rules of the church, than the victim. The callous and insensitive responses sounded like the words issued by COGIC's Presiding Bishop in October 2007, when clergy sexual abuse issues begin to gain attention.

"We now live in a litigious society. People file lawsuits for every conceivable grievance, whether real or imagined. To protect the name, image, and assets of the Church of God in Christ, we must take positive steps to seriously investigate very case of alleged sexual abuse by the clergy. We must stand behind and support those who are falsely accused of sexual improprieties and found innocent by the courts. We must also insure that the Church act quickly to take firm and positive action against those who violate the sanctity of their positions and are found guilty of sexual abuse and other sexual improprieties."

Although, he was no longer connected to the COGIC community he grew up in, Davis said the plight of the victims and the cloud of darkness compelled him to move forward to uncover the truth.

In May 2012 I began a series of interviews with this victim. The victim has long been a member of various COGIC and non-COGIC churches as a musician. The victim provided a fairly detailed account of abuse he had endured beginning at the age of 6 and continuing through becoming an adult. According to victim's testimony, abuse in COGIC began at St. John's church at the age of 12. For this individual, the cycle of church abuse began with a minister who at first was musically connected to the victim but soon this connection led into sexual activity which continued over several years. In addition to the victim's adolescent involvement with the aforementioned minister, testimony of involvement with an elder involved with numerous musical groups, an adult church musician, a minister and an adult church lay member were all detailed. Of the five noted pedophiles, three were members of St. John's and two members of Wilborn's Temple at the time of the abuse in the mid-1970's. Abuse by the elder involved with numerous musical groups began at the age of 14 years old and involved not only the abuser and the abused but other adults and minors as well. The abuse victim states that he was introduced to orgies in the loft at Garland Brothers Funeral Home."

Despite the evidence, after the meeting, Davis discovered Bishop Wright was unsympathetic to the victims. He wrote, "Based on the previous day's meeting with Superintendent Clark having disclosed additional issues with the offending pastor I was quite confident that Bishop Wright had to be aware of these issues as well. In the end, Bishop Wright stated that his concern was exposing the church (COGIC) to a lawsuit from the pedophile and that the jurisdiction didn't have money to deal with the victims anyways. Completely disgusted with the response from Bishop Wright I alerted him of my resolve to contact the national church organization and that I would bring this issue to the forefront in the coming months."

Depending on the outcome of the case, COGIC, Inc could be facing for the first time a federal level investigation into child sex crimes. In October last year a Kansas City Catholic bishop was arrested for failing to report *suspected* child sexual abuse.

(m) Denver police arrested a 26-year-old youth minister with St. John's Church

Colorado: 2010: Denver police arrested a 26-year-old youth minister with St. John's Church of God in Christ after a 15-year-old member accused him of sexual assault.

MacFranklin Alexander, of 4800 Hale Parkway, faces charges of felony sexual assault on a child, sexual assault on a child by one in a position of trust and sexual assault on a child involving a pattern of conduct.
Alexander is accused of having ongoing sexual contact with the girl for about three months,

Keeping our Children Safe from sexual predators

said Lt. John Priest of the Denver Police Department's Crimes Against Persons Bureau. "This individual has known the victim for some time," Priest said. "He is the minister of music for the church and deals with young people." Investigators do not believe that Alexander, who was arrested Wednesday, was involved with any other children in the congregation, and he does not have a history of sexual abuse convictions. Priest would not comment on where the alleged assaults took place.

The head minister of St. John's Church of God in Christ, Jay Betts, was not available for comment Thursday. But the spiritual leader of the Church of God in Christ denomination for the state of Colorado, Bishop Frank Johnson, said he was looking into Alexander's arrest. Johnson said he was not sure if Alexander was a licensed member of the clergy or simply a member of the congregation who has the title of minister.

"We won't tolerate anything like that," Johnson said. "He can't have anything to do with the church if he has been accused of something like this."

Johnson said the Church of God in Christ is a Pentecostal denomination with 53 churches in Colorado.

St. John's Church of God in Christ is a tiny congregation with just a handful of members, said Pastor Phil Campbell of Park Hill Congregational Church at 2600 Leyden Street.

For the past few years, Campbell's church has been renting space to St. John's Church of God in Christ because it does not have its own

Keeping our Children Safe from sexual predators

building. Members of the church use one of Park Hill Congregational's Sunday school classrooms for their weekly services and a Wednesday evening Bible-study session. "They are kind of like what people describe as a storefront church except they don't have a storefront," Campbell said. "When they have big gathering, about 20 people gather." Campbell said he does not know Alexander well. He said he doesn't have any reason to believe that the assaults took place in the church.
http://www.topix.com/forum/county/brevard-fl/T20GF7RM646SDKTC0

By Bob Allen

(N)Missouri Baptist Convention officials are watching a member church whose pastor was arrested recently on sexual abuse charges a year after his previous acquittal of child molestation.

Travis Smith, 42, of California, Mo., appeared for arraignment Oct. 16 in Moniteau County court. He faces charges of forcible rape, statutory rape and sexual abuse alleged to have occurred in 1998, statutory rape in 1999 and statutory rape and sodomy in 2005.

Smith, pastor of First Baptist Church in Stover, Mo., since 2006, was found not guilty on Sept. 28, 2011, by a jury in Morgan County of misdemeanour child molestation of a 14-year-old girl in 2009. A separate charge of statutory

Keeping our Children Safe from sexual predators

rape was dropped because that accuser turned out to have been 17, the age of consent in Missouri, rather than 15 as first claimed when their alleged improper relationship began.

Posted: Wednesday, July 11, 2012 8:37 pm | *Updated: 2:22 am, Sun Jul 15, 2012.*

www.wavenews.com: Opinion: In Inglewood, accused pastor is suddenly the man nobody knows By Betty Pleasant, Contributing Editor

(O)While the Rev. Gordon Solomon was busy last Friday pleading not guilty to charges that he "substantially" sexually abused a child, people who used to know him suddenly never heard of him and the Inglewood church he pastored became a Southland tourist's Mecca as everyone flocked to it.

According to the District Attorney's Office, the 50-year-old Solomon, a native Belizean, was arrested on or about the Fourth of July and charged with nine felony counts of committing lewd acts on a 14-year-old girl who attended his church — acts which began in June 2010 when the child was 12 and did not end until July 1, 2012, when the child's mother stumbled upon explicit text messages Solomon allegedly sent the girl. The mother immediately summoned police who confiscated the lewd missives and set about building the case against him.

(P) UPDATE: Gallia Pastor Arraigned on 20 Sexual Abuse Charges UPDATE: Gallia Pastor Arraigned on 20 Sexual Abuse Charges
10/22/12 @ 11:15 a.m.

GALLIPOLIS, Ohio (WSAZ) -- A Pastor is facing 20 counts of unlawful sexual conduct with a minor.

Pastor David A. Young, of Simpson Chapel United Methodist Church in Rio Grande, Ohio, was arraigned Monday morning in Gallia County.

Young was arrested Oct. 16 in connection with the charges.

The alleged victim is a teenager between the ages of 13 and 14-years-old who knew Young as part of a class that Young taught through the church.

Young entered a plea of not guilty to all 20 counts. Bond was set at $250,000 and Young is not to have any contact with the victim.

Assistant Prosecutor Britt Wiseman had request a bond of $500,000 because of the numerous counts. Wiseman said the incidents happened over a period of 1 year -- between September 25, 2011 and September 25, 2012.

A few members of the congregation were in the courtroom in support of their pastor. Tom Weaver was one member and says the church is going through a time of difficult healing.

Keeping our Children Safe from sexual predators

Purpose of Child Safety education and training: To empower children, families, and communities to learn better ways of reducing child exploitation and victimization from sexual predators in Community; to train, educate, and inform Parental and Community on a child's personal safety

What you need to know about Sexual offenders

If we're going to protect our children from sexual offenders, then we must educate ourselves. We have to understand the mind of a sexual predator. It is not enough to periodically check the sex offender lists that our state maintains. We must be proactive.

Sex Offenders seek out children because they are easy prey and vulnerable. It is easy to win a child's trust. They start out slowly and work their way into the mind of child. They typically don't even have to use force to manipulate a child to do what they want. We, as citizens, parents, and educators, have to teach our children about these sexual offenders. Let's begin:

- Talk to your child about sexual offenders.
- Explain to your child about what sexual offenders could do. (Even children as young as three or four can be taught.)
- Teach your child that their body is private, and that they must not let someone touch their private parts.

Keeping our Children Safe from sexual predators

- Teach your children that they shouldn't undress in front of someone even if that person appears to be nice to them
- Teach them to immediately tell you if someone tries to touch them, asks them to undress, tries to undress them, or tries to get them to touch that person.
- Give your children lots of good attention. Spend time with them. Talk with them.
- Teach them not to give out any personal information about themselves or others in their family.
- Help them understand the difference in going to someone like a police officer or teacher for help and going to someone else, who really wants to harm them
- Practice role-playing so that your child is prepared in case he is approached by a potential child sex offender.

Keeping our Children Safe from sexual predators

How to Help Missing and Exploited Children

1. Check sex offender lists, and everyone should do so periodically to stay abreast of just who is living in your neighborhood and community.
2. If you suspect that a child is being abused, contact your local law enforcement agency immediately.
3. If you have any doubts about what you are seeing, write everything down so that it is fresh in your memory, and you can easily recall it as you inform your local police.
4. If you think you have seen a child that has been listed on an Amber Alert, access the Amber Code Website immediately, as well as your local law enforcement agency.
5. You can also use the link at CodeAmber that allows anyone to email the details of an alert to anyone else they know, wherever they live.
6. The list offenders who have committed sex crimes continue to grow.

Child Safety: Don't

1. Never leave your child unsupervised in a public place or even in your front yard.
2. Don't allow your child to roam the neighborhood by herself or even walk down the street alone
3. Don't leave your child at places, such as, public parks, video arcades, even the mall.

Keeping our Children Safe from sexual predators

4. Be sure you talk to your child about your child body, and the right not to be touched.
5. Continue to educate your child as he/she grows, and start early.

Characteristic of a child predator

1. Child predators are typically afraid of adult intimacy
2. Child predators search out children who are vulnerable and easily manipulated
3. Child predator generally needs to control others
4. Child predators may have been abused as a child.
5. Child predators often has a great desire for power
6. Child predators typically have a low self esteem
7. Child predator are afraid of adult intimacy, so they search out children, who are easily manipulated
8. A Child predator usually refuses to take responsibility for his actions

Do you know how many children will be sexually victimized before adulthood?

Statistics show that 1 in 5 girls and 1 in 10 boys will be victimized before they reach adulthood.

Juveniles as Victims

Violent Crime Victimization

Q: How does offender age vary with victim age in
sexual assault?

A: Young juveniles (under the age of 12) are most
likely to be sexually assaulted by persons under
age 18.

Percent of all sexual assault offenders, 2008

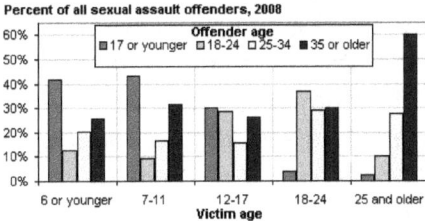

Note: Data are from law enforcement agencies in
35 states and the District of Columbia.

Older juveniles (ages 12 to 17) are nearly as likely
to be sexually assaulted by young adults (ages 18
to 24) as by persons under age 18 Internet
citation: *OJJDP Statistical Briefing Book*. Online.
Available:
http://www.ojjdp.gov/ojstatbb/victims/qa02401.asp
Released on December 21, 2010.

Adapted from Snyder, H. & Sickmund, M. (2006).
*Juvenile Offenders and Victims: 2006 National
Report*, Chapter 2. Washington, D.C.: Office of
Juvenile Justice and Delinquency Prevention.

Data Source: National Archive of Criminal Justice
Data. *National Incident-Based Reporting System,
2008: Extract Files* [Computer file]. Ann Arbor, MI:
Inter-university Consortium for Political and Social
Research [distributor], 2010-08-13.

Children of Victory: More Facts you need to know

<u>Child Safety Facts:</u>

- Over 56,000 cases of child sexual abuse were reported and substantiated in 2007.[1]
- As many as one in three girls and one in seven boys will be sexually abused at some point in their childhood.[2]
- In as many as 93% of child sexual abuse cases, the child knows the person that commits the abuse.[3]
- Most perpetrators are acquaintances, but as many as 47% are family or extended family.[4]
- Approximately 30% of cases are reported to authorities

What is child sexual abuse? Child sexual abuse is any form of sexual activity imposed upon a child by an adult or other child in a position of power, authority, or influence. Child sexual abuse can involve touching the intimate parts of a child's body, enticing or forcing the child to have sexual relations, or participating in non touching offenses, such as obscene phone calls or taking pornographic photos.

The child victim may be a boy or girl; in most cases knows and trusts the abuser; may be an infant, toddler, preschooler, or school-aged child up to age 18; may come from any socioeconomic background, ethnic, or religious group; is usually afraid to tell about the sexual abuse for fear of being blamed or punished; and rarely is abused by a stranger.

Who sexually abuses children? The people who sexually abuse can be immediate or extended family members (fathers, mothers, stepparents, grandparents, siblings, uncles, aunts, cousins, etc.). They can be neighbors, babysitters, religious leaders, teachers, coaches, or anyone else who has close contact with children.

Warning signs that might suggest someone is sexually abusing a child: The following behaviors could be cause for concern:

- Making others uncomfortable by ignoring social, emotional, or physical boundaries or limits.
- Refusing to let a child set any of his or her own limits. Using teasing or belittling language to keep a child from setting a limit.
- Insisting on hugging, touching, kissing, tickling, wrestling with, or holding a child even when the child does not want this physical contact or attention.
- Turning to a child for emotional or physical comfort by sharing personal or private information or activities that are normally shared with adults.
- Frequently pointing out sexual images or telling inappropriate or suggestive jokes with children present.
- Exposing a child to adult sexual interactions without apparent concern.

Keeping our Children Safe from sexual predators

- Having secret interactions with teens or children (e.g., games; sharing drugs, alcohol, or sexual material) or spending excessive time e-mailing, text-messaging, or calling children or youth.
- Being overly interested in the sexuality of a particular child or teen (e.g., talks repeatedly about the child's developing body or interferes with normal teen dating).
- Insisting on or managing to spend unusual amounts of uninterrupted time alone with a child.
- Seeming "too good to be true" (e.g., frequently babysits different children for free, takes children on special outings alone, buys children gifts or gives them money for no apparent reason).
- Frequently walking in on children/teens in the bathroom.
- Allowing children or teens to consistently get away with inappropriate behaviors.

If you observe these behaviors in someone you know, talk to that person. For more information and guidance about starting a conversation with someone, visit the Stop It Now! Online help center or calls the national, toll-free Helpline at (888) PREVENT.

Warning signs in children of possible sexual abuse: Stop It Now! Has developed a tip sheet to help identify possible warning signs. Any one sign does not mean that a child was sexually abused, but the presence of several

suggests that you begin asking questions and
consider seeking help.

Behaviors you may see in a child:

- Has nightmares or other sleep problems
  without an explanation
- Seems distracted or distant at odd times
- Has a sudden change in eating habits
- Refuses to eat
- Loses or drastically increases appetite
- Has trouble swallowing.
- Sudden mood swings: rage, fear,
  insecurity, or withdrawal
- Leaves "clues" that seem likely to
  provoke a discussion about sexual
  issues
- Writes, draws, plays, or dreams of
  sexual or frightening images
- Develops new or unusual fear of certain
  people or places
- Refuses to talk about a secret shared
  with an adult or older child
- Talks about a new older friend
- Suddenly has money, toys, or other gifts
  without reason
- Thinks of self or body as repulsive, dirty,
  or bad
- Exhibits adult-like sexual behaviors,
  language, and knowledge

If you have questions or would like resources
or guidance for responding to a specific
situation, visit the Stop It Now! Online help
center or calls the national, toll-free Helpline at
(888) PREVENT.

Keeping our Children Safe from sexual predators

Materials:

- The Joyful Child Foundation Be Safe, Be Brave: A Parent's Guide to Prevention. Most parents find themselves horrified by the prospect that someone they trust could violate their children, and it is our natural inclination to believe that it could not have already happened and gone unnoticed. This realization is often followed by disbelief, fear, and even hopelessness. This handbook is designed to aid you in protecting your children against sexual abuse and abduction.

- National Center for Missing & Exploited Children Child Safety Resources: Parents, guardians, and adults who care for children face constant challenges when trying to help keep children safer in today's fast-paced world. The National Center for Missing & Exploited Children (NCMEC) offers easy-to-use safety resources to help address these challenges. For decades, children were taught to stay away from "strangers." But this concept is difficult for children to grasp, and often the perpetrator is someone the child knows. It is more beneficial to help build children's confidence and teach them to respond to a potentially dangerous situation, rather than teaching them to look out for a particular type of person. NCMEC's prevention and safety education programs and materials contain information and tips that will help you keep your children safer. The Just in Case... and Know the Rules publication series are especially important for parents and guardians.

STOP IT NOW! Parents & Caregivers: Do Your Part to Protect Kids. Don't wait until you see a problem before you start taking action to protect kids. Learn some simple things you can do every day to make sure kids are safe, and then teach others. Make sure every adult who cares about kids has the information they need to be confident about making a commitment to safety. You can begin prevention today.

- Learn to Recognize Warning Signs
- Learn Everyday Actions to Keep Kids Safe
- What Parents Need to Know When Selecting a Program for a Child

More Child Safety Facts:

- Approximately, 1.8 million adolescents in the United States have been the victims of sexual assault.[7]
- 33% of sexual assaults occur when the victim is between the ages of 12 and 17.[8]
- 82% of all juvenile victims are female.[9]

Keeping our Children Safe from sexual predators

- Teens 16 to 19 years of age were 3 1/2 times more likely than the general population to be victims of rape, attempted rape, or sexual assault.[10]
- 69% of the teen sexual assaults reported to law enforcement occurred in the residence of the victim, the offender, or the residence of another individual.[11]
- Approximately 1 in 5 female high school students report being physically and/or sexually abused by a dating partner.[12]
- Approximately 1 in 7 (13%) youth Internet users received unwanted sexual solicitations.[13]
- 4% of youth Internet users received aggressive solicitations, in which solicitors made or attempted to make offline contact with youth.[14]
- 9% of youth Internet users had been exposed to distressing sexual material while online.[15]

Warning Signs in Children and Adolescents of Possible Sexual Abuse: Stop It Now! has developed a tip sheet (PDF) to help identify possible warning signs. Any one sign does not mean that a child was sexually abused, but the presence of several suggests that you begin asking questions and consider seeking help.

- Behavior you may see in a child or adolescent: as nightmares or other sleep problems without an explanation
- Seems distracted or distant at odd times
- Has a sudden change in eating habits
- Refuses to eat

Keeping our Children Safe from sexual predators

- Loses or drastically increases appetite
- Has trouble swallowing.
- Sudden mood swings: rage, fear, insecurity, or withdrawal
- Leaves "clues" that seem likely to provoke a discussion about sexual issues
- Writes, draws, plays, or dreams of sexual or frightening images
- Develops new or unusual fear of certain people or places
- Refuses to talk about a secret shared with an adult or older child
- Talks about a new older friend
- Suddenly has money, toys, or other gifts without reason
- Thinks of self or body as repulsive, dirty, or bad
- Exhibits adult-like sexual behaviors, language, and knowledge

Behavior more typically found in adolescents:

- Self-injury (cutting, burning)
- Inadequate personal hygiene
- Drug and alcohol abuse
- Sexual promiscuity
- Running away from home
- Depression, anxiety
- Suicide attempts
- Fear of intimacy or closeness
- Compulsive eating or dieting

If you have questions or would like resources or guidance for responding to a specific situation, visit the <u>Stop It Now! Online help center</u> or call the national, toll-free Helpline at (888) PREVENT.

Materials:

- The <u>NetSmartz Workshop</u> is an interactive, educational safety resource from the <u>National Center for Missing & Exploited Children</u> (NCMEC) and Boys & Girls Clubs of America for children aged 5 to 17, parents, guardians, educators, and law enforcement that uses age-appropriate, 3-D activities to teach children how to stay safer on the Internet.

- <u>NetSmartz Teens</u>: Today's teens have knowledge of the Internet that often surpasses that of their parents. Because so many teens are Internet-savvy, it is imperative that they also have an understanding of the dangers that exist online and how to deal with them. Watch teens share their own "Real-Life Stories" about issues affecting them on the Internet, such as cyberbullying, online enticement, and giving out too much personal information.

- NCMEC's <u>Prevention and Safety Education</u> programs and materials contain information and tips that will help you keep children and teens safer.

Keeping our Children Safe from sexual predators

- Teen Victims Project: Teen Tools Sexual Assault Fact Sheet (PDF): The National Center for Victims of Crime has developed a series of Teen Tools fact sheets, written for teens, about how to recognize a crime, what emotions to expect, and how to receive or give help.

- Understanding Teen Dating Violence Fact Sheet (PDF): The Centers for Disease Control's National Prevention Center for Injury Prevention and Control developed a fact and resource sheet to help families understand and prevent teen dating violence.

Additional Resources:

- CyberTipline: NCMEC operates the CyberTipline as a means of reporting incidents of child sexual exploitation, including the possession, manufacture, and/or distribution of child pornography; online enticement; child prostitution; child sex tourism; extrafamilial child sexual molestation; unsolicited obscene material sent to a child; and misleading domain names, words, or digital images. The CyberTipline is staffed 24 hours a day, 7 days a week. Make a report at www.cybertipline.com or by calling 1.800.THE.LOST if you have information that will help in our fight against child sexual exploitation.

Keeping our Children Safe from sexual predators

- The National Center for Victims of Crime is dedicated to forging a national commitment to help victims of crime rebuild their lives. The National Center's toll-free Helpline, (800) FYI-CALL, offers supportive counseling, practical information about crime and victimization, and referrals to local community resources, as well as skilled advocacy in the criminal justice and social service systems.

- If you or someone you know needs help or support, call the National Sexual Assault Hotline, (800) 656-HOPE, operated by The Rape, Abuse & Incest National Network (RAINN). Your call is anonymous and confidential. You may also contact a counselor using the National Sexual Assault Online Hotline. The online hotline provides live, secure, anonymous crisis support for victims of sexual assault, their friends, and families. Both resources are free of charge and are available 24 hours a day, 7 days a week. If you would like to search for a specific crisis center in your area, visit http://centers.rainn.org.

References

1. Kilpatrick, D., Acierno, R., Saunders, B., Resnick, H., Best, C., Schnurr, P. "National Survey of Adolescents." Charleston, SC: Medical University of

South Carolina, National Crime Victims Research and Treatment Center, 1998.

2. "Sexual Assault of Young Children as Reported to Law Enforcement: Victim, Incident, and Offender Characteristics." U.S. Department of Justice, Bureau of Justice Statistics, 2000.

3. "Sexual Assault of Young Children as Reported to Law Enforcement: Victim, Incident, and Offender Characteristics." U.S. Department of Justice, Bureau of Justice Statistics, 2000.

4. Bureau of Justice Statistics. "National Crime Victimization Survey." U.S. Department of Justice, 1996.

5. "Sexual Assault of Young Children as Reported to Law Enforcement: Victim, Incident, and Offender Characteristics." U.S. Department of Justice, Bureau of Justice Statistics, 2000.

6. Silverman, J. G., Raj, A., Mucci, L. A., and Hathaway, J. E. "Dating Violence Against Adolescent Girls and Associated Substance Use, Unhealthy Weight Control, Sexual Risk Behavior, Pregnancy, and Suicidality." Journal of the American Medical Association, Vol. 286, (No. 5), 2001.

7. Wolak, J., Mitchell, K., Finkelhor, D. Online Victimization of Youth: Five Years Later, National Center for Missing & Exploited Children, 2006. Available online: http://www.missingkids.com/en_US/public ations/NC167.pdf.

8. Ibid.

Keeping our Children Safe from sexual predators

Create a Family Safety Plan

- NetSmartz Workshop is an interactive, educational safety resource from NCMEC and Boys & Girls Clubs of America for children aged 5 to 17, parents, guardians, educators, and law enforcement that uses age-appropriate, 3-D activities to teach children how to stay safer on the Internet and in the real world.

Additional Resources:

- CyberTipline: NCMEC operates the CyberTipline as a means of reporting incidents of child sexual exploitation, including the possession, manufacture, and/or distribution of child pornography; online enticement; child prostitution; child sex tourism; extrafamilial child sexual molestation; unsolicited obscene material sent to a child; and misleading domain names, words, or digital images. The CyberTipline is staffed 24 hours a day, 7 days a week. Make a report at www.CyberTipline.com or by calling (800) THE-LOST if you have information that will help in our fight against child sexual exploitation.

- Darkness to Light programs raise awareness of the prevalence and consequences of child sexual abuse by educating adults about the steps they can take to prevent, recognize, and react responsibly to the reality of child sexual abuse.

- The Safer Society Foundation, Inc., a nonprofit agency, is a national research, advocacy, and referral center on the prevention and treatment of sexual abuse.

- Stop the Silence aims to increase awareness about and conduct programming to address the prevention and treatment of child sexual abuse and the relationships between this issue and broader societal violence.

- RadKIDS® is a national leader in children's safety education and provides a holistic, practical, and realistic life skills safety program available for children and parents.

- NAPSAC, the National Association to Prevent Sexual Abuse of Children is dedicated to ending childhood sexual abuse in three generations through awareness, education, and the advocacy of children's rights.

References

1. Child Maltreatment. Administration for Children and Families, U.S. Department of Health and Human Services. 2007. Available online:

Keeping our Children Safe from sexual predators

http://www.acf.hhs.gov/programs/cb/pubs/cm07/cm07.pdf.

2. Briere, J., Eliot, D. M. "Prevalence and Psychological Sequence of Self-Reported Childhood Physical and Sexual Abuse in General Population: Child Abuse and Neglect," 2003, 27:10.
3. Douglas, Emily, and Finkelhor, D., Childhood sexual abuse fact sheet, http://www.unh.edu/ccrc/factsheet/pdf/childhoodSexual AbuseFactSheet.pdf, Crimes Against Children Research Center, May 2005.
4. Briere, J., Eliot, D. M. "Prevalence and Psychological Sequence of Self-Reported Childhood Physical and Sexual Abuse in General Population: Child Abuse and Neglect," 2003, 27:10.
5. Finkelhor, D. "The Prevention of Childhood Sexual Abuse." Future of Children, 2009; 19(2):169–94.
6. Stop It Now, available online: http://www.stopitnow.org/behaviors_watch_adult_with_children.

Keeping our Children Safe from sexual predators

What should I do if my child is a victim of sexual exploitation?

If your child indicates that he or she may have been the victim of sexual exploitation or abuse, follow the steps noted below. After you've done that, take a look at the Do's and Don'ts list we've provided.

- Seek appropriate medical attention to be sure your child has not been physically injured
- Report the exploitation to your local law-enforcement agency
- Inform child-protection, youth-services, child-abuse, or other appropriate social-service organizations about the exploitation
- Seek counseling or therapy for your child
- Contact the National Center for Missing & Exploited Children at 1-800-843-5678 or www.cybertipline.com to find out what resources are available to you

Do

- Respect your child's privacy
- Support your child and the decision to tell you
- Show physical affection, and express your love and confidence with words and gestures
- Explain to your child that he or she has done nothing wrong

Keeping our Children Safe from sexual predators

- Remember that children seldom lie about acts of sexual exploitation
- Keep the lines of communication open with your child

Don't

- Panic or overreact to the information disclosed by your child

- Criticize or blame your child

Chapter III ICAC: Internet Crimes Against Children

Reference:
Teen Safety Information Hwy;NCMEC
Net Cetera: Chatting with kids about being Online
Keeping Kids Safer on the Internet, NCMEC, OJJDP
Children as Target of Internet Crimes-who is vulnerable?

OVC, Director Gillis states: "Youth are often curious and eager to try new things. Many youth struggle with issues of rebellion and independence and seek attention and affection from people outside the home, often by using computers. For predators, the Internet is a new, effective, and more anonymous way to seek out and groom children for criminal purposes such as producing and distributing child pornography, contacting and stalking children for the purpose of engaging in sexual acts, and exploiting children for sexual tourism for personal and commercial purposes.

Internet Crimes Against Children: A Need to Know

Movies: A Must See For Parents & Teens:
1. Trust
2. Trade
3. Taken

UNICEF estimates that there are more than4 million websites featuring sexually exploited minors. Further, the number of child pornography websites is growing: 480,000 sites were identified in 2004 compared to 261,653 in 2001.

More than 200 new images are circulated daily, and UNICEF estimates that the production and distribution of child pornographic images generates in between 3 and 20 billion dollars a year.

United Nation released a report in July 2009 asserting that there are approximately 750,000 sexual predators using the internet to try to make contact with children for the purpose of sexually exploiting them

The NCMEC, National Center for Missing & Exploited Children maintains the CyberTipline, an online reporting system for (internet service providers) ISPs and the public to report online child pornography.

Keeping our Children Safe from sexual predators

www.cybertipline.com or Toll Free Phone #:1-800-843-5678
www.cybercrime.gov/rules/kiinternet.htm and www.cybercrime.gov/rules/lessonplan1.htm
www.ftc/gov/bcp/conline/pubs/online/sitesee.htm: kidz privacy
www.cybercitizenship.or/aboutus/aboutus.html: Cybercitizen Awareness Program:

www.fbi.gov/publication/pguide/pguidee.htm: Parent's guide to Internet Safety
Resource:
National Center for Missing & Exploited Children is a comprehensive resource for families, victim service practitioners, and law enforcement personnel.

US Department of Justice's Office of Juvenile Justice and Delinquency Prevention (OJJDP) and functions as a clearinghouse and resource center for collecting and distributing information about missing runaway, and sexually exploited children, including exploitation resulting from Internet solicitations.

Other Partners: US Postal Inspection Service, US customs Service and FBI.

www.missingkids.com/cybertip: Cybertip Child Pornography Tipline: 1-800-843-5678.

Internet Crimes against Children: Task Force Program: Regional Resource for assistance to parents, educators, prosecutors, law enforcement personnel and others who work on child victimization issues.

Types of Internet Victimization
- Enticing them through online contact for the purpose of engaging them in sexual acts.
- Using the Internet for the production, manufacture, and distribution of child pornography.
- Using the Internet to expose youth to child pornography and encourage them to exchange pornography.
- Enticing and exploiting children for the purpose of sexual tourism (travel with the intent to engage in sexual behavior) for commercial gain and/or personal gratification.

Keeping our Children Safe from sexual predators

Survey areas:

Sexual solicitation: request to engage in sexual activities

1. Aggressive sexual solicitation: mail/telephone in person or request on line contact
2. Unwanted exposure to sexual material-pictures naked people or people having sex
3. Harassment: Threats or other offensive content
4. 1-5 youth received a sexual approach or solicitation via internet

Statistical Findings

1. 1-5 youth received a sexual approach or solicitation over the internet in the past year.
2. 1 in 33 youth received an aggressive sexual solicitation in the past year. This means a predator asked a young person to meet somewhere, called a young person on the phone, and/or sent the young person correspondence, money, or gifts through the US Postal Service.
3. 1 in 4 youth had an unwanted exposure in the past year to pictures of naked people or people having sex.
4. 1 in 17 youth was threatened or harassed in the past year.

Ref. OVC, Office Victim & Crimes, Internet Crimes Against Children.

Keeping our Children Safe from sexual predators

More Statistical Data

One in five U.S. teenagers who regularly log on to the Internet says they have received an unwanted sexual solicitation via the Web. Solicitations were defined as requests to engage in sexual activities or sexual talk, or to give personal sexual information.

Crimes Against Children Research Center:

- 25% of children have been exposed to unwanted pornographic material online.
  - Crimes Against Children Research Center

- Only 1/3 of households with Internet access are actively protecting their children with filtering or blocking software.
  - Center for Missing and Exploited Children

- 75% of children are willing to share personal information online about themselves and their family in exchange for goods and services.
  - eMarketer

- Only approximately 25% of children who encountered a sexual approach or

Keeping our Children Safe from sexual predators

solicitation told a parent or adult.
- Crimes Against Children Research Center

- One in 33 youth received an aggressive sexual solicitation in the past year. This means a predator asked a young person to meet somewhere, called a young person on the phone, and/or sent the young person correspondence, money, or gifts through the U.S. Postal Service.
- Your Internet Safety Survey

- 77% of the targets for online predators were age 14 or older. Another 22% were users ages 10 to 13.
- Crimes Against Children Research Center

Keeping our Children Safe from sexual predators

Glossary of terms:
www.onguardonline.gov. Net Cetera:
OnGuard Online: Stop. Think. Click.

1. Avatar-A graphic alter ego you create to use online; can be a 3D character or a simple icon, human or whimsical.

2. Blocking software-A program to filter content from the internet and restrict access to sites or content based on specific criteria

3. Chat room-An online space where you can meet and exchange information through messages displayed on the screens of others who are in the room.

4. COPPA- children's Online Privacy Protection Act: It gives parents control over what information websites can collect from their kids under 13

5. Cyber bullying-Bullying or harassment that takes place online; includes posting embarrassing pictures or unkind comments on a person's profile or sending them via instant message or email.

6. Hacking-Breaking into a computer or network by evading or disabling security measures.

7. Security software-identifies and protects against threats or vulnerabilities that may compromise your computer or your personal

Keeping our Children Safe from sexual predators

information; includes anti-virus and anti-spyware software and firewalls.

8. Sexting-Sending or forwarding sexually explicit pictures or messages from a mobile phone.

9. Spyware-Software installed on your computer without your consent to monitor or control your computer use.

10. Texting-Sending short messages from one mobile phone to another.

11. Tween-when a child is between 8-12 years old

12. Phishing-when scam artists send spam, pop-ups, or text messages to trick you into disclosing personal, financial, or other sensitive information.

13. Peer-to Peer (P2P) file sharing-Allows you to share files online-like music, movies, or games-through an informal network of computers running the same sharing software.

14. Instant messaging (IM)-enables two or more people to chat in real time, and notifies you when someone on your buddy list is online.

15. Virtual world- a computer simulated online place where people use avatars-graphic characters-to represent themselves.

Keeping our Children Safe from sexual predators

16. Webcam-a video camera that can stream live video on the web; maybe built into the computer or purchased separately.

Keeping our Children Safe from sexual predators

What are some of the primary dangers children and teens face on the Internet?

First: What you need to know about "Grooming"

Grooming is a process that predators used to create a form of manipulation-an emotional psychological dependence; to encourage children to have sex with online enticement. It begins with selection child's desired behaviors or psychology characteristic-low self esteem or family problems.

The predator promote intra-familiar rifts; alienate children from others; assume parental role in declaring their love to them; infatuation simultaneously; introduce child pornography to the child; Grooming is a seduction methodology; children are shown nudity, sexual abuse, suggestive images; sending children sex toys; demonstrate indoctrinate children; children in the process provide information and compromise themselves-in the end, predators threatens to expose victim to friends and family, may sometime threatened their life and/or their family.

The victim is shown a high level of attention, affection, empathy, and generosity, mastering music, movies, games appeals to the children.

The primary dangers that children and teens face on the Internet are child predators, Internet artifacts, "sexting" and cyber bullies.

Keeping our Children Safe from sexual predators

"Sexting" is a term which describes the act of attaching a pornographic image to a text message. Both adults and children engage in this behavior; however, it is illegal to create, possess or distribute a pornographic (nude, semi-nude, engaged in sex) image of a child under the age of 18. Typically, teenage girls who engage in this behavior are attempting to gain the attention of a teenage boy and believe that the act will entice, show interest or demonstrate commitment. Unfortunately, teens involved in relationships eventually break up and the inappropriate images that were meant for a single person can be distributed to many people. Exam: NY Congressman

Cyber bullies are people who utilize the Internet, computers or cell phones to tease, embarrass, intimidate, humiliate, harass or threaten another person. This act has become a significant problem among children who choose the Internet as a tool for harassment because they believe that they are anonymous and cannot be identified. Law enforcement typically becomes involved in cyber bully cases when there is a threat of violence to a minor. Exam: Mom pretended to be a teen boy contact via internet to her daughter former female friend-pretending that she/he had a crush on the girl. The girl committed suicide because the boy broke up w/her via internet.

Child predators: use a process called "grooming" to control or manipulate children. Steps within the grooming process involve the child predator taking actions that can be detected, such as sending gifts to gain a child's trust. Strangers who send gifts are a warning sign. Child predators also attempt to erode barriers and convince children to break rules that would otherwise protect a child from harm (for example: Don't talk to strangers; tell parents where you are going; don't leave the house after parents have gone to bed." These rules are obstacles to gaining access to a child so a child predator will attempt to convince a child to start breaking the rules to facilitate future access.

Other resources:
www.missingkids.com
www.meganslaw.ca.gov
www.cybertipline.com
www.isafe.org
www.NetSmartz.org
www.safekids.com
www.safeteens.com
www.webwisekids.org.
http://www.gems-girls.org/

A Must Read: Be Informed: Recent News from DOJ

CHILD PORNOGRAPHY CASES: DOJ & HOMELAND SECURITY
RECENT NEWS REPORTS: JULY 2011

WASHINGTON – *Attorney General Eric Holder and Department of Homeland Security (DHS) Secretary Janet Napolitano announced today*

Keeping our Children Safe from sexual predators

the unsealing of three indictments and one complaint charging a total of 72 individuals for their participation in an international criminal network dedicated to the sexual abuse of children and the creation and dissemination of graphic images and videos of child sexual abuse throughout the world. Attorney General Holder and Secretary Napolitano announced the charges with Assistant Attorney General Lanny A. Breuer of the Justice Department's Criminal Division, Director of U.S. Immigration of Customs Enforcement (ICE) John Morton and U.S. Attorney Stephanie Finley of the Western District of Louisiana.

Operation Delego, an ongoing investigation that was launched in December 2009, targeted the 72 charged defendants and more than 500 additional individuals around the world for their participation in Dreamboard – a private, members-only, online bulletin board that was created and operated to promote pedophilia and encourage the sexual abuse of very young children, in an environment designed to avoid law enforcement detection.

To date, 52 of the 72 charged defendants have been arrested in the United States and abroad. Members traded graphic images and videos of adults molesting children 12 years-old and

176

under, often violently, and collectively created a massive private library of images of child sexual abuse. The international group prized and encouraged the creation of new images and videos of child sexual abuse – numerous Dreamboard members sexually abused children, produced images and videos of the abuse, and shared the images and videos with other members of Dreamboard.

Operation Delego represents the largest prosecution to date in the United States of individuals who participated in an online bulletin board conceived and operated for the sole purpose of promoting child sexual abuse, disseminating child pornography and evading law enforcement.

"The members of this criminal network shared a demented dream to create the preeminent online community for the promotion of child sexual exploitation but for the children they victimized, this was nothing short of a nightmare," said Attorney General Holder. "This operation marks another important step forward in our work to protect children across - and beyond - this country. Our nation's fight to protect the rights, interests, and safety of children goes on, and it will continue to be a top priority of this Justice Department."

Keeping our Children Safe from sexual predators

FBI, Special Agent Greg Wing inferred that "It is believed that more than half a million pedophiles are online every day." Pedophiles go where children are. Before the Internet, that meant places such as, amusement parks and zoos. Today, the virtual world makes it alarmingly simple for pedophiles-often pretending to be teens themselves-to make contact with young people.

Keeping our Children Safe from sexual predators

Most effective way to protect children from Internet:

1. Maintain open and honest constructive communication
2. Make children aware of the threats and the consequences for inappropriate behavior.
3. If a child's actions are possibly increasing the risk and putting them in danger, monitoring software program can be an effective tool.
4. Parents need to educate themselves: Google can be used as to the various websites; face book www.allfacebook.com
5. Keep computer in a centralize location of the home-never allow your child to have a computer in their room.
6. www.cybertipline.com if there is child/teen victimization

Chapter IV   **Human Child Trafficking**

Child Human Trafficking Hot line:
1-800-655-4095
1-888-428-7581
Reference: Understanding child trafficking:
Training manual to fight trafficking in children
for labor, sexual and other forms of Exploitation
www.unicef.org
www.usdoj.gov/crt/crim/tpwetf.htm
US Department of Justice & U.S. Department
of Labor

Human Trafficking is Illegal: Say No to Modern
Day Slavery: Federal laws prohibit Sex
Trafficking and Trafficking in persons for forced
labor and Mistreatment. New Laws provide
options for Trafficking victims regardless of
Immigration status. If someone is being forced
to work or held against their will we can help. It
is illegal to use force or threats to make
someone work to pay off a debt.

Human Trafficking is "Modern Day Slavery."
Trafficking of children is defined as the
recruitment, transportation, transfer, harboring,
or receiving of children for the purpose of
exploitation-by force, against their will. It is
about selling our children for sex and force
labor. It is the threats, use of force and other
forms of coercion, abduction, fraud, deception-
telling families and children - lies of a "better
life."

Child human trafficking is a Human right issue-
it is a violation of Children's rights and could be

an issue of national security. In total it is the profit from exploitation of prostitution-sexual exploitation, force labor, slavery, forced servitude and sometimes removal of organs. Child human trafficking is an abuse of power given for receipt of payment of our children.

Child Human Trafficking consists of Coercion, Fraud, and Force:

Coercion: Threats of harm to the victim and/or victim's family through intimidation, shame and embarrassment of revealing their part in commercial sex. It is emotional psychological verbal abuse; nights of quotas, rewards, punishment, lying about police arrest and threats of deportation.

Force: This is about restricting their movement; physical and sexual abuse; beatings and slapping; burning, repeated rapes, to create submission and confinement to residence;

Fraud: This is false promises of a better life from boyfriend and/or Caretaker.

Reports have revealed the following states and cities which are practicing the fastest criminal enterprise of Child human trafficking:

In California

Sacramento is one of the leading cities for Child Human Trafficking; Oakland, San Diego and LA.

Keeping our Children Safe from sexual predators

Other Cities/States Active in Child Human Trafficking:

1. Atlanta
2. Chicago
3. Detroit
4. Seattle
5. Washington DC
6. New York
7. New Jersey
8. Texas
9. Connecticut
10. Maryland
11. Louisiana

According to Nicholas D. Kristof, New York Times....

"Girls are not locked in cages. Rather, they're often runaways out on the street wearing short skirts or busing out of low cut tops, and many Americans perceive them not as trafficking victims but as miscreants who have chosen their way of life. So even when they're 14 years old, we often arrest and prosecute them- even as the trafficker goes free." Kristof continues: "Teenage girls on American streets may appear to be selling sex voluntarily, but they're often utterly controlled by violent pimps who take every penny they earn."

Commercial sexual exploitation of children can take many forms, including forcing a child into prostitution, [1] other forms of sexual activity, or child pornography. Child exploitation can also include forced labor or services, slavery or practices similar to slavery, servitude, the removal of organs, illicit international adoption, trafficking for early marriage, recruitment as child soldiers, for use in begging, as athletes (such as child camel jockeys or football players), or for recruitment for cults.[2]

According to "Make Way Partners," January 2008,

- There are at least 30 million victims of modern day slavery in the world today (US trafficking in Person Report).
- Each year it is estimated that there are 1 million new victims of human trafficking (the US Department of State).
- Estimates as high as 80% of trafficking victims are women and over 50% in slavery are children (US Government).
- Some reports have stated human trafficking generates approximately $9.5 billion each year; other reports are even higher-32 billion a year.
- The US is the number one country of destination for trafficked victims. The land of the free and the home of the brave have become the receiving country for sex slaves and forced manual workers.
- Run-away or kidnapped children are also sold and exploited within our borders and Internet child pornography or solicitation is thriving (www.makewaypartner.or/effects.html).
- Rising tide of human trafficking by Americans against other Americans

Keeping our Children Safe from sexual predators

between 1.3 million and 2.8 million runaways and homeless youths living on America's streets are one of the most at risk populations for exploitation (PR Newswire)

A Need to know:

- Girls as young as 5 years old have been sold. Anyone is at risk because the victims have been men or women
- It is happening on all seven (7) Continents
- Most victims are shipped out and never heard from again. Some killed and other brain washed into thinking it is a normal life style. The very few that return to normal lives, have a difficult time living a normal life.
- The victims are recruited by being tricked/deceived into traveling to other countries with men/women because of high paying jobs, such as modeling, office work etc. Also they are paid to go to the countries sometimes by boyfriends and girlfriends.
- Victims are not criminals-they are forced to these things: Tricked/deceived-a violation of trust.

Keeping our Children Safe from sexual predators

People Involved in Child Human Trafficking: Who are they?

1. Document providers
2. Family members
3. Friends
4. Transporters
5. Intermediaries
6. Corrupt officials
7. People contributing with the intent to exploit, recruit
8. Employers or trafficking of children
9. Institutional Players: Corrupt police; government officials and many others

20 Ways You Can Help Fight Human Trafficking

After first learning about human trafficking, many people want to help in some way but do not know how. Here are just a few ideas for your consideration.

1. Learn human <u>trafficking red flags and ask follow up questions</u> so that you can detect a potential trafficking situation.
2. In the United States, report your suspicions to law enforcement at 911, Department of Justice at 1-888-428-7581, and the National Human Trafficking Resource Center at 1-888-3737-888. Victims, including undocumented individuals, are eligible for services and immigration assistance.
3. Be a conscientious consumer. Make socially responsible investments. Let

your favorite retailers know that you support their efforts to maintain a slavery free supply chain. Encourage your company or your employer to take steps to investigate and eliminate human trafficking throughout its supply chain and to publish the information for consumer awareness. Refer to the Department of Labor's List of Goods Produced by Child Labor or Forced Labor.

4. Hire trafficking survivors.
5. Volunteer your professional services to help an anti-trafficking organization that need help from lawyers, doctors, dentists, counselors, translators and interpreters, graphic designers, public relations and media professionals, event planners, and accountants.
6. Donate funds or needed items to an anti-trafficking organization.
7. Organize a fundraiser and donate the proceeds to an anti-trafficking organization.
8. Join or start a grassroots human trafficking coalition.
9. Encourage your local schools to include modern slavery in their curriculum. As a parent, educator, or school personnel, be aware of how traffickers target school-aged children.
10. Meet with and write to your local, state and federal government representatives to let them know that you care about combating human trafficking in your community.

Keeping our Children Safe from sexual predators

11. Create and distribute public awareness materials such as t-shirts, posters, and public service announcements for radio. Or distribute already existing materials available from the Department of Health and Human Services or Department of Homeland Security.
12. Host an awareness event to watch and discuss a recent human trafficking documentary. On a larger scale, host a human trafficking film festival. Several noteworthy films and documentaries have been produced in the last several years that bring attention to the plight of victims worldwide.
13. Write a letter to the editor for your local paper about human trafficking in your community.
14. Incorporate human trafficking information into your professional associations' conferences, trainings, manuals, and other materials as relevant.
15. STUDENTS: Join or establish a university club to raise awareness about human trafficking throughout the local community and identify victims. Request that human trafficking be an issue included in such university courses as health, migration, human rights, social work, and crime. Increase scholarship about human trafficking by publishing an article, teaching a class, or hosting a symposium.

Keeping our Children Safe from sexual predators

16. COMMUNITY ORGANIZATIONS: ensure that your staff is able to identify and assist trafficked persons.
17. LAW ENFORCEMENT OFFICIALS: join or start a local human trafficking task force.
18. MENTAL HEALTH OR MEDICAL PROVIDERS: extend low-cost or free services to human trafficking victims assisted by nearby anti-trafficking organizations.
19. IMMIGRATION ATTORNEYS: learn about and offer to human trafficking victims the immigration benefits for which they are eligible.
20. EMPLOYMENT LAW ATTORNEYS: look for signs of human trafficking among your clients.

Chapter V   **Violent acts/Severe parental supervision neglect leading to a child's death.**

Aggravated Abuse to a child leading to death:

Severe Neglect-improper parental supervision nearly five children die every day in America from abuse and in 2010, an estimated 1,560 children died from abuse and neglect in the United States. [2]

In the same year, Children's Advocacy Centers around the country served over 266,000 child victims of abuse, providing victim advocacy and support to these children and their families. In 2011, this number was over 279,000. [3] 2010 NATIONAL ABUSE STATISTICS [2]

Approximately 695,000 children were victims of maltreatment (unique instances). 47 states reported approximately 3.4 million children received preventative services from Child Protective Services agencies.

Children younger than one year had the highest rate of victimization of 20.6 per 1,000 children in the population of the same age. Of the children who experienced maltreatment or abuse, over 78% experienced neglect; more than 17% were physically abused; just under 10% were sexually abused; approximately 8% were psychologically maltreated; just over 2%

were medically neglected; and approximately 10% experienced other types of maltreatment.

Nearly 80% of reported child fatalities as a result of abuse and neglect were caused by one or more of the child victim's parents. 2011 CHILDREN'S ADVOCACY CENTER STATISTICS [3]

Among the over 259,000 children served by Children's Advocacy Centers around the country during 2011, some startling statistics include:

- 106,522 children were ages 0 to 6 years.
- 99,624 children were ages 7 to 12 years.
- 69,372 children were ages 13 to 18 years.
- 187,862 children reported sexual abuse.
- 48,264 children reported physical abuse.
- 179,014 children participated in forensic interviewing at a Children's Advocacy Center.

Among the over 226,000 alleged offenders investigated for instances of child abuse from January through June 2011, some startling statistics include:

- 146,981 were 18+ years old.
- 24,075 were ages 13 to 17 years.
- 17,250 were under age 13 years.
- 88,182 were a parent or step-parent of the victim.

Keeping our Children Safe from sexual predators

- 47,096 were related to the child victim in another way.
- 71,877 were an unrelated person the victim knew.

[1] Every Child Matters Education Fund (2009). We Can Do Better: Child Abuse and Neglect Deaths in the US. http://www.everychildmatters.org/storage/documents/pdf/reports/wcdbv2.pdf

[2] U.S. Department of Health and Human Services: Administration for Children & Families. Child Maltreatment 2010. http://www.acf.hhs.gov/programs/cb/pubs/cm10/cm10.pdf

[3] National Children's Alliance 2011 national statistics and 2010 national statistics collected from Children's Advocacy Center members.

Chapter V1   Solutions

"Working together protects children."
To reduce children being exploited and victimized we need to actively support raising awareness. "Awareness is our best defense."
We can do this by the following:

1. Training and teaching Child Safety Advocates to be the extra eyes and ears in the community and in their city to better protect children.
2. Child Safety education and training in community, parents, caregivers and children.
3. Increase Child Safety education/training in the public schools, parks, community centers-any where children congregate.
4. Child Safety Resource Centers located throughout the city, county and state; teaching parents proper parental supervision; providing Child Safety education and training including prevention, protection, and Child

Keeping our Children Safe from sexual predators

Safety strategies for parents/children/guardians and communities.via CD, books, flyers, pamphlets etc. to include outreach to various cultural and ethnic groups.

Movies: A Must See For Parents & Teens:
Trust
Trade
Taken

Reference:
Predator Criminal Investigators
1. FBI, Crimes Unit against Children: Civil Rights Unit
2. US Attorney General: DOJ
3. ICE, Immigration & Customs
4. Homeland Security
5. Task Force: LA, San Diego & Sacramento
   www.dhs.gov/humantrafficking
   www.ourborder.ning.com www.ice.gov.
6. Training Manual to fight trafficking of Children, labor, sex and other forms of exploitation.
7. Read: US State Department Human Trafficking report: June 29, 2011.
8. Niolas Alipuri, Director of Program Division, UNICEF.
9. Palermo Protocol.

10. TV PA-Trafficking victim Protection 2000, 03, 05, 2008.
11. UC Berkley Human Rights Center, Free Denied, Force Labor.

About COV

COV Mission statement: Children of Victory mission is the Safety and Well-being of Children. Our commitment is to educate and train community, parents, and children; provide community-grass root and school based child safety literature, activities etc; in addition to developing collaborative partnerships with County, City, State, and Federal Law Enforcement Agencies, schools and other child centered organizations- to reduce child exploitation and victimization. As a result, child safety education and training will help bring community awareness and help teach others to be the extra "Eyes and Ears" in the community (as well as on-line) to better protect and keep our children safe from sexual predators.

COV Objectives:
1. To help improve the knowledge, self-confidence, and assertiveness skills of children: Outcome: they will be safer because the will be better able to recognize danger and resist potential offenders.
2. To reduce child exploitation and victimization
3. To help enhance children's sense of self-worth.

Keeping our Children Safe from sexual
predators

4. Provide opportunities to practice safety
skills and habits

Teach child safety education to families,
children, parents, caregivers, grandparents,
guardians, teachers, pastors and the entire
church body.

Clearly, COV Goals:

- Help minimize the opportunity and risks to harm children
- Teach and educate how to practice child safety skills
- Teach children how to be alert and recognize potential risks
- Teach children it is ok to say "No." Shout it out loud and run!
- Teach children the difference between "Good touch, Bad touch."
- Inform parents and children on child safety rules

COV Child Safety Focus: What is it? What does it mean?

COV 5-fold Strategy Focus:

1. Missing and Exploited Children
2. Sexual Crimes against Children
3. Internet Crimes against Children
4. Human Child Trafficking
5. Physical acts of Violence & Severe Neglect that leads to a child's death
6. Child Safety Parental supervision/ training

Keeping our Children Safe from sexual predators

COV Child Safety Foundational principles are committed to the safety and well being in reducing child exploitation and victimization.. It is about the protection of our children and providing a unique opportunity for all of us to act together as a community, a city, a state a nation to protect our innocent ones COV Child Safety focus is about helping children grow up in a safe loving environment from sexual predators in the neighborhood/community as well as on-line.

COV child Safety focus emphasizes teaching and education children/parents/families and community on how we can keep children safe from sexual predators.

COV Child Safety is about distribution of child safety literature in community, schools, parks and recreation centers.

COV Child Safety is about implementing preventive measures to protecting our children by recruiting and training Community Child Safety Advocates to be the extra "Eyes and Ears" in the community to keep our children safe.

COV is about reducing potential dangers or/and potential risks

Community Partnerships: A Powerful Alliance

Working closely with and developing Community Partnership with law enforcements agencies, Probation Department, School

Keeping our Children Safe from sexual predators

officials, Children Social services while the LAPD, LASD deal with these crimes against children issues on a daily basis. Since 2001, COV is continuing to serve the families of Los Angeles in a variety of ways:

1. Conducted multiple meetings/workshops in Los Angeles, Hollywood, Culver City, Inglewood City Hall, and East Los Angeles.
2. Collaborative Community Partnerships:
   - LAPD
   - LA County Sheriff Department,
   - California DOJ (Department of Justice)
   - NCMEC, Center for Missing and Exploited Children,
   - Steve Cooley, Los Angeles District Attorney's Office,
   - Los Angeles County Probation Department
   - LAUSD
   - LA County DCFS and many other Local agencies
   - Federal agencies: FBI, Los Angeles: US Marshal, Los Angeles:

COV Community Involvement

1. Literature distribution of the Safety and well-being of Children
2. Reducing child victimization by training Community Child Safety Advocates

Keeping our Children Safe from sexual predators

3. Providing Education and Training to Community by conducting Community Workshops
4. Host of weekly Child Safety Radio Program

Child Safety Education & Distribution
Child Safety Education/Training, Training and Developing Community child Safety Advocate, and Distribution of Child Safety Literature

Promotion and Community Awareness

Community Workshops; weekly Child Safety Radio program; literature distribution, Press Release, Newsletters, PSA, Child Safety News Reports via Radio, Television and Cable Television:

Weekly Radio Child Safety Program: KTYM: 1460 AM: Thursday 5:00 pm.

Community Child Safety Webinars

Literature distribution in schools, park/recreation centers and neighborhood-door to door

Top Priority: Community Awareness: Community/training workshops, preventative child safety education, providing child safety information and distribution of child safety literature. Help reduce, prevent child victimization by being the "Extra Eyes and Ears" in the community.

Keeping our Children Safe from sexual predators

COV Objectives.

- Teach child safety education to families, children, parents, caregivers, grandparents, guardians, teachers, pastors and the entire church body.
- To help improve the knowledge, self-confidence, and assertiveness skills of children: Outcome: they will be safer because the will be better able to recognize danger and resist potential offenders.
- To reduce child exploitation and victimization
- To help enhance children's sense of self-worth.
- Provide opportunities to practice safety skills and habits

Department of Justice: Solution to Child Exploitation

*"The solution to child exploitation must also include **prevention through public awareness and education** campaigns. It must also include deterrence using tools like sex offender monitoring. And, law enforcement must have the technological tools you need to investigate these crimes. The Department is taking a number of steps to help on each of these fronts."*

Keeping our Children Safe from sexual predators

Note: The following post appears is adapted from the remarks of Acting Deputy Attorney General Gary G. Grindler, who spoke today at the National Internet Crimes Against Children's Conference in Jacksonville, Florida.

About MC:

A Time to share: An Overnighter that involved sexual abuse: At the tender age of 7 years old, and a 2nd grader; MC suffered sexual abuse while staying overnight with her best girl friend. As she was asleep, she was awakened by the Abuser who was the uncle of her friend.
MC never told anyone until 50 years later.

MC Griffin Campbell, (MA, M.Div.) is the President & Founder of (COV) Children of Victory, a nongovernmental, nonprofit Child Safety Advocate organization. She is also a pastoral therapist, speaker, teacher and writer.

In 2007, she was awarded (Los Angeles Child Safety Advocate Certification) by Los Angeles CA. Mayor Antonio Villaraigosa. MC works in and throughout the community of Los Angeles County; Los Angeles City, City of Moreno Valley and Riverside County.

MC has a working relationship with community leaders; in additional to works with LA City Councilman, Tom LaBonge, Los Angeles County Sheriff Department, and Los Angeles Police Department and other child safety related organizations.

Keeping our Children Safe from sexual predators

MC also host her own weekly radio child safety program that focus on teaches listeners the importance of the safety and well being of our children. Her program reaches out to listeners throughout the state of California.

MC is married to husband Gene. They have 4 adult children, 9 grandchildren, 1 great grand daughter. They live in Los Angeles California. www.childrenofvictory.com

About Children of Victory

Children of Victory (COV) is a 501(c)(3) nonprofit, grass root, child safety advocacy organization, that works with the Los Angeles County Sheriff Department, Los Angeles Police Department, and many other agencies that focus on Missing & Exploited Children, Sexual Assaults against Children, Internet Crimes against Children, Human Child trafficking, and Aggravated Child Abuse is committed to Community

Child Safety Training and Education to parents, guardians and children; in addition to On-Line Child Safety training and awarding Certificates to Community Child Safety Advocates to be the extra "Eyes and Ears" in the community to better protect children from predators. Since its establishment in 2001, COV has conducted multiple community workshops in and throughout Los Angeles City, County; in addition to, Riverside County. COV has

Keeping our Children Safe from sexual predators

trained hundreds of community child safety advocates. For more information, call 323-382-4364 or visit website: www.childrenofvictory.com

CONTACT:
COV Media
323-382-4364
Fax #: 323-927-1711

www.ingramcontent.com/pod-product-compliance
Lightning Source LLC
Chambersburg PA
CBHW071529040426
42452CB00008B/946